MY FATHER'S SMOKEHOUSE

Stories and Recipes from Fishcamp

VIVIAN FAITH PRESCOTT

ALASKA
NORTHWEST
BOOKS®

Library of Congress Cataloging-in-Publication Data

Names: Prescott, Vivian Faith, author.
Title: My father's smokehouse : stories and recipes from fishcamp / Vivian Faith Prescott.
Description: [Berkeley] : Alaska Northwest Books, [2022] | Includes bibliographical references. | Summary: "A collection of short stories and recipes shared from a family fishcamp on Wrangell Island. The book explores the author's way of life as she uses traditional Tlingit and Sámi knowledge to care for the people and the world around her"-- Provided by publisher.
Identifiers: LCCN 2021045202 (print) | LCCN 2021045203 (ebook) | ISBN 9781513128610 (paperback) | ISBN 9781513128627 (hardback) | ISBN 9781513128634 (ebook)
Subjects: LCSH: Tlingit Indians--Food--Alaska--Wrangell. | Tlingit Indians--Alaska--Wrangell--Social life and customs. | Indian cooking. | Wrangell Island (Wrangell, Alaska)--Social life and customs.
Classification: LCC E99.T6 P74 2022 (print) | LCC E99.T6 (ebook) | DDC 979.8004/9727--dc23/eng/20211014
LC record available at https://lccn.loc.gov/2021045202
LC ebook record available at https://lccn.loc.gov/2021045203

LS2022

Published by Alaska Northwest Books®
an imprint of

WEST
MARGIN
PRESS
WestMarginPress.com

WEST MARGIN PRESS
Publishing Director: Jennifer Newens
Marketing Manager: Alice Wertheimer
Project Specialist: Micaela Clark
Editor: Olivia Ngai
Design & Production: Rachel Lopez Metzger

To my dad, Mickey Prescott
and
to my children
Vivian Mork Yéilk', Mitch Mork, Breanne Pearson, and Nikka Mork

CONTENTS

ACKNOWLEDGMENTS

Gunalchéesh, Shtax'héen Ḵwáan, for allowing me to live at my fishcamp, Mickey's Fishcamp, in Ḵaachxaana.áak'w, Wrangell, near Ḵeishangita.aan ("Red Alder Head Village").

Gunalchéesh to the Kiks.ádi, Naanyaa.aayí, Kaach.àdi, Kayaashkiditaan, S'iknax.ádi, Xook'eidí, Kaasx'agweidí, and Taalḵweidí Clans. I acknowledge I'm a guest here in Tlingit Aaní and I write these words on your precious land.

First of all, I want to thank my dad, Mitchell Prescott, aka Mickey, for accompanying me on this fishcamp journey. Thank you for sharing your knowledge, especially your fishing secrets. Thank you for being willing to learn along with me and for taste-testing all my recipes.

Gunalchéesh, giitu, and much gratitude to my sister Tracey Prescott Martin for writing, transcribing, and taste-testing my fishcamp recipes, and for collecting my father's recipes. Without you, this project would've been overwhelming. Thank you to Vivian Mork Yéilk' for her consulting work on Tlingit culture, language, and harvesting protocols. Gunalchéesh, X'unei Lance Twitchell, for your assistance with the sound charts. Your work with the revitalization and preservation of the Lingít language is invaluable. Also, thank you to Vincent Balansag and Lynn Torres Balansag for sharing your fish head soup recipe. And my deepest thanks to all you Wrangellites who've enjoyed my photos and writing over the years. Thank you for reading and for inspiring me to write about our island life.

Many thanks to Mary Catherine Martin for encouraging me to share my life at Mickey's Fishcamp in the *Juneau Empire*'s *Capital City Weekly*, where versions of the chapters in this book first appeared. It's great to have someone believe in your writing. Thank you to my Planet Alaska column editors at the *Capital City Weekly* over the years: Clara Miller, Mary Miller, and Ben Hohenstatt. The essay "The Underside of Leaves" first appeared in *Alaska Women Speak*, a great little Alaskan literary journal. I offer profound thanks to my husband, poet Howie Martindale, for his editing skills. And to my many, many grandkids, and great-grandchildren, these stories and recipes are for you. When I'm long gone you can mix some berries into a batch of cookies, or toss in some spruce tips, and you'll think of me. You come from a long line of camp cooks who toss in a little bit of this and a bit of that and then cook it up in the hopes it tastes good. (It usually does, but not always.)

Gunalchéesh, Kiara Shea Meissner, for contributing your map art for this book. Kiara is a Tlingit artist from Wrangell, Alaska, who operates a graphic arts business called On The River. After a book is written, there's more work to do before we hold it in our hands, and I appreciate the experts at West Margin Press. Much gratitude to editor/publisher Jennifer Newens for encouraging me to include my recipes in this foodoir and for her recipe-editing expertise. And giitu to editor Olivia Ngai, copy editor Emily Bowles, and designer Rachel Metzger for making this book magic happen.

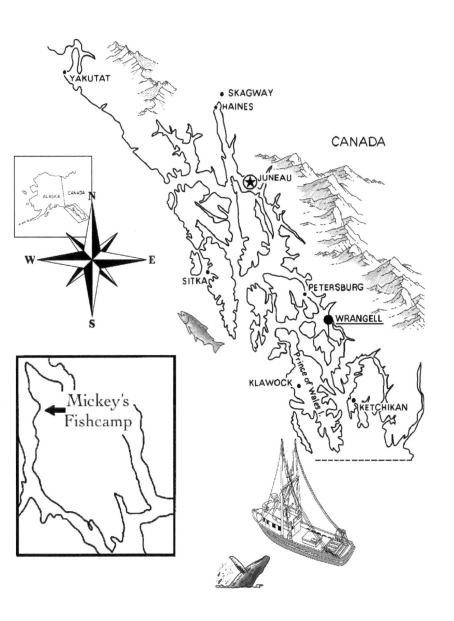

INTRODUCTION:
SENSE OF TIME,
SENSE OF SEASONS

Living with nature every day is my life story. The landscape is filled with stories, waiting beside our smokehouse or beneath a patch of devil's club, hiding under a frond of sea lettuce, or rolling on an old cottonwood log in front of fishcamp. The Stikine Wilderness and the Tongass National Forest are a part of my life here in Southeast Alaska, where I'm a guest of the Shtax'héen Ḵwáan, the Stikine Tlingit. The stories I'm offering in this book come from life at and near my fishcamp—Mickey's Fishcamp, named for my dad. Our fishcamp is in Ḵaachxaana.áak'w, the Tlingit name for Wrangell, near Ḵeishangita.aan, meaning "Red Alder Head Village," today called Shoemaker Bay.

In order to live in this landscape, I need to know the signs nature sends me. I take notice when bear activity begins in the spring because the spruce roots are ready. I notice the first heavy spring fog because I should then begin to look for fiddlehead ferns, salmonberry shoots, and fireweed. The first skunk cabbage sprouting up from the warm earth says king salmon are coming. And in the fall, after the first frost, it's time to harvest Hudson Bay tea. In this worldview, the landscape measures time by the fluid motion of trees, water, new shoots, and animal activities.

When traveling and living in Tlingit country, Tlingit Aaní, it's important to understand the Tlingit calendar begins a new year

US Forest Service Sign, erected on Wrangell Island in the Tongass National Forest by Mickey Prescott when he worked for the Forest Service as a field supervisor.

in July with Xáat Dís, the Salmon-Return Moon, also called the Fattening Moon, Gataa Dís. The month names describe an intimate knowledge of the Southeast Alaska landscape. For example, in the Stikine regional calendar, December, Saanáx Dís (Through-the-Head Moon), is when hair grows on the heads of seals in the womb, and March, Héen Taanáx Kayaaní Dís (Underwater-Plants-Sprout-Moon), is when underwater plants bud and seaweed grows on rocks.

The Tlingit calendar is dependent upon what subsistence activities are occurring during the month. It is a calendar of motion, of doing, of being. However, since each community in Tlingit Aaní is unique, each community's calendar varies according to what nature in that geographic area is doing at a particular time; for example, Wrangell's Tlingit calendar in the Stikine region differs from the calendar of the village of Klukwan.

The Tlingit calendar contains the ecological Traditional Knowledge of my children's ancestors, evident in the detail. Tlingits have thrived here by acquiring the medicinal knowledge of the plants, by knowing and adapting sustainable harvesting methods, and by passing down stories about taboos and proper behavior while interacting with the landscape. The sea, beaches, mountains, trees, plants, animals, and even mosquitoes are interwoven into the Tlingit worldview. This worldview is still present in my children's lives and their children's lives.

Through continued interaction with the landscape, my grandchildren's Tlingit cultural identity is formed and reinforced. Their ancestral relationship to place strengthens relationships in our ever-changing world. This knowledge about the land and sea is what I try to give my children and grandchildren. My children adopted me into their T'aḵdeintaan Clan and gifted me the name Yéilk' Tlaa, meaning "Mother-of-Cute-Little-Raven," and my family and I are learning about those traditions and worldviews. Myself, my children, and grandchildren are Sámi too; we have ancestors who were Indigenous People from Sápmi, which includes parts of Norway, Finland, Sweden, and Russia. Many Sámi traditions were not brought over to this country, but some worldviews stayed with the Sámi diaspora. One is the báiki, a Sámi concept meaning we carry a sense of home within us that endures. This is living at fishcamp: báiki.

In Sámi culture we have eight seasons, with seasons in between the traditional four seasons. For instance, in Sápmi there's a winter–spring season, gidádálvve, around March–April, and even a summer-autumn season, tjaktjagiesse, around August. I prefer the idea of more seasons because it means paying closer attention to what's going on in nature around me.

There are eight seasons at Mickey's Fishcamp too. Four seasons are not enough. But what could I call them? Harvesting, traveling the logging roads, having picnics, smoking fish, jigging for halibut, picking spruce tips, and picking huckleberries, blueberries, and salmonberries all happen so naturally it's hard to think of these activities as separate. Indigenous Peoples put knowledge together to understand, whereas Western thinking takes things apart to understand.

If I created a fishcamp calendar, our seasons would begin in the spring with March–April.

HINT SEASON: In March we head to the beach to harvest popweed (bladderwrack, abundant in Southeast Alaska) and wait for herring and hooligan (a type of smelt). There's a hint of spring in the air: the smells change, the sun gives a bit of warmth. We are excited.

RETURN SEASON: April is the season of beginnings, when everything returns: light, birds, plants. We harvest plant shoots when they first emerge from the earth. Sandhill cranes and snow geese return to the river flats.

ROOTS AND SHOOTS AND BUDS SEASON: May is when we are rooting in the dirt, harvesting roots and shoots and tips. The weather is good enough to fish for salmon and start jigging for halibut. Whales appear!

BLOOM SEASON: Salmonberries are the first berry. Depending on where you live in Southeast Alaska, they typically ripen mid to late June. Blueberries start showing up in certain areas. Thimbleberries blossom.

CELEBRATION SEASON: July is a celebration of berries and fish. We pick berries, fish, pick berries, fish... repeat. Again and again. All our berries are ripe and we're hard at work, picking.

PREPARE AND ENJOY SEASON: In August and September we catch the last of the halibut, smoke the salmon, catch fall coho salmon, and pick fall berries: gray currants, red huckleberries, cranberries, and lingonberries. We smoke and jar the salmon and freeze the berries and make jelly and jams with them. We start hunting deer.

TRAVELING AND TRAVERSING SEASON: We hunt for deer and moose in October and November. It's the last chance to travel the logging roads and hike the forests before it snows.

STORYTELLING AND EXPERIMENTING SEASON: December through February are about food, recipes, and art. We snowplow the walking path for the community. It is also gifting season.

The way I structure the chapters in this book allows you to see *what* is harvested and *when*.

It is how I live, following the cues nature gives. The Tlingit subsistence calendar begins in July during salmon season; however, I open the first chapter of this book in the spring and continue according to the fishcamp calendar. I take you through two subsistence cycles (two harvesting years), though the seasonal stories do not move through linear time. Using this structure, a grandson might appear older in one chapter and younger in another.

I also omit deer and moose hunting stories. Those activities have slowed down for me as I've aged and mostly consist of driving the logging roads *looking* for moose or deer. Our sons-in-law provide us with deer meat. Someday, I will return to smoking and jarring deer meat. And because of the limited space in these pages, I didn't include all the varieties of berries, shoots, medicines, or seaweeds we harvest. Maybe that'll be another book.

Why include recipes? We live a mostly subsistence life in Wrangell, so it's only natural to develop our own ways of preparing food; at the same time, we rely on the knowledge of our fellow Wrangellites and our own traditions to grace our tables and fill our bellies. I was inspired to include recipes because whenever I share a photo of a dish on social media that includes spruce tips or goose tongue, people want to know more. Also, I started listing all the things one could make from the foods we were harvesting, like red huckleberries or spruce tips, which intrigued my friends and followers. Therefore, Dear Reader, I gift you recipes in this book, though I am not a chef. I consider myself an average cook. What I am, though, is someone who is curious and adept at fishcamp gastronomy.

The stories don't exactly follow the fishcamp calendar order, but it's close. At fishcamp, one of our values is flexibility. Whatever is blooming or emerging or ripening in nature is what we're going to be harvesting or cooking and preparing. When we hear fishermen are catching cohos nearby, we head out. When there's a sunny day, we take advantage of the weather to pick berries. When it's cloudy, we go pick thimbleberries because they get really mushy in the heat and they're soggy in the rain. Many times I have had to adjust my writing schedule because of a harvesting or fishing opportunity, which are dependent on the tides and the weather. My body is in tune with this island rhythm. I can't separate myself from

Mickey's Fishcamp in Wrangell, Alaska, K̲aachx̲aana.áak'w, near K̲eishangita.aan, "Red Alder Head Village."

this island. It's me. At night, when the house smells like spruce tips or smoked salmon and I'm tucked under my covers and the dogs are sleeping on the floor beside me, I open my window and let the ocean's scent in. Sometimes I can hear the roar of a sea lion or a loon cry or the crackly squawk of a blue heron. As sleep comes upon me, I am part of an eagle's downy feather falling to earth or the nudge of waves against my seawall.

So, Dear Reader, as you go harvesting with me through these pages and spend time making art or listening to a story, be willing to learn and be inspired. Get to know me and my dad, my dogs, my children and grandchildren. Get to know our old logging road system, meandering the hundred-plus miles across our island shaped like a snow goose, and get to know my little fishcamp at the edge of the sea.

Any mistakes with the Lingít and Sámi language and cultural knowledge are mine. Any mistakes with the science, history, or gastronomy are mine. Please forgive me.

SEA AND FOREST SEASONING

MAKES 1 SMALL (4-OUNCE) JAR

My first gift to you. The flavors in this seasoning blend perfectly, like the sea meeting the forest edge. The salty seaweed mixes with the tang of pine from the spruce tips. This seasoning can be used in soups, on fish or egg dishes, and more. Adding chili powder, cumin, or some chipotle spice will contribute heat. Be sure to experiment with this recipe according to your own palate. Adjust sugar or spice content according to your taste.

2 teaspoons sugar

1 teaspoon garlic powder

1 teaspoon freshly ground
black pepper

1 teaspoon paprika

¼ cup dried and finely chopped
goose tongue (beach plant)

¼ cup finely chopped dried red
seaweed or orange popweed

¼ cup finely chopped dried
spruce tips

½ teaspoon sea salt or Spruce Tip
Salt (page 20)

Mix the sugar, garlic powder, black pepper, paprika, goose tongue, seaweed, spruce tips, and salt together in a small bowl. Using a spoon or funnel, pour the seasoning mixture into a small Mason jar. Poke holes in the lid to use as a shaker. (You can also wash out and recycle old spice containers.)

SPRUCE TIP JUICE & SALT

Dear Reader, before you read any further you should know I'm obsessed with spruce tips. I love picking them, sniffing them, eating them, drinking them, and cooking with spruce tips. As you'll see, spruce tips and spruce tip juice, pulp, and salt are in many of the fishcamp foods I prepare.

Spruce Tip Juice is the remaining liquid after spruce tips are steeped in a pot and strained out. Don't throw away the strained spruce tip pulp, though—that also freezes beautifully and can be used in many recipes.

To make Spruce Tip Juice, simmer 4 cups of water with 2 cups of spruce tips for 20 to 30 minutes, then strain out the spruce tips. Freeze the juice and pulp in separate containers to use later. The juice will stay fresh for up to a year.

Spruce Tip Salt is an essential fishcamp seasoning and is easy to make. Some people peel off the needles and discard the stem before chopping up the tips, but I use the whole spruce tip and bring out the food processor to do the work. Spruce tip salt is best made with fresh spruce tips, but frozen spruce tips are fine too.

To make Spruce Tip Salt, pour ½ cup sea salt and ½ cup chopped spruce tips into a medium bowl and mix with clean hands or a spatula. Spread the salted spruce tips out in a single layer on two sheet pans. Let the mixture dry for a couple days in a sunny place, tossing every few hours, or dry in a dehydrator or a preheated oven at 150°F with the door cracked open. When the spruce tip salt is completely dry, store the salt in a Mason jar or sealable plastic bags.

FIRST FISHCAMP CYCLE

SKUNK CABBAGE:
A HARBINGER OF SPRING

We arrive at the Tongass National Forest sign. The pavement
ends here and before us are a hundred miles of old logging roads.
My dad is a retired field supervisor with the US Forest Service, so
he's familiar with these roads. We often plan excursions to learn,
photograph, and harvest from nature, loading up his truck with
binoculars, a rifle, and our lunch. We are here on this early spring
day to look for skunk cabbage. My father claims skunk cabbage
is a sign it's time to go out and fish for "spring kings," meaning
king salmon, which is his real motive for taking me on this
mini-adventure.

Snow melts, rotten leaves become soil, streams rush, plants push,
and the ground warms. A bright yellow plant sprouts up.

Rainforest crocus, muskeg lantern, and swamp lantern are
other names for Western skunk cabbage, *Lysichiton americanus.*
In Lingít, it's called x̱'áal'. Skunk cabbage is a cornlike stalk with
a bright yellow hood and big, green waxy leaves that are a foot
and a half to over four feet high. At the top of a single tall stem
is the plant's spadix. Resembling a corn cob, the spadix contains
hundreds of tiny flowers and is shrouded by a bright yellow hood,
the spathe.

*Skunk cabbage scent attracts beetles and flies. Pollen collects
on their feet and wings as they fly from flower to flower
and plant to plant, scattering flower dust.*

As my dad navigates the truck down the muddy road, we point out to each other the telltale yellow of the emerging skunk cabbages in ditches and along hillsides. I'm looking to photograph larger plants. I roll down the truck window and smell the scent of skunk cabbage. Though people describe it as a mixture of skunk, carrion, and garlic, I find it enticing. To me, it smells like spring. My dad turns to me and says, "I ate some skunk cabbage as a kid. I even tried the leaves. They don't taste good." I laugh because I tried it as a kid too and thought the same thing.

My memory takes me down another dirt road in Wrangell, on the hill behind town. My sister was five years old and I was four, and we were exploring our neighborhood as we often did. "Wild corn!" we shrieked when we spotted the yellow blooms of what was actually skunk cabbage. A friend had told us it was wild corn. What did we know? Yes, we'd heard it called skunk cabbage, but the only skunk I'd ever seen was in a cartoon. Maybe skunks ate corn, we reasoned. We slid down the embankment into the ditch where the yellow stalks were. My sister snapped off a stalk for herself and I broke one off for myself. I stood in my rubber boots, ankles deep in black muck. Corn was our favorite, so I eagerly took a bite.

Immediately a bitter, burning sensation stung my lips and tongue. Beside me, my sister was spitting and wiping her mouth. We scrambled out of the ditch and ran crying toward home. My parents made us drink milk. The milk cuts the bitter, peppery flavor somewhat, but I still tasted that nasty stuff for a week.

*Deer walks gingerly, pressing her hooves into the muck.
She nibbles the tip of the new growth.*

Unlike humans, deer and bear eat parts of the skunk cabbage raw. Skunk cabbage provides them with high-protein food, a perfect springtime meal after a long winter. Deer nip off the tops of new growth and bears will eat the roots to help clean out their systems after emerging from hibernation. Canada geese love the summer leaves. Humans have to be careful, though, because calcium oxalate crystals make skunk cabbage inedible to us in its raw form: the taste is sometimes described to be like eating needles.

The nightly frost is gone, the warm sun beckons, bears emerge from dens.

We carefully drive a few more miles, running into snow and ice on the road and keeping a lookout for skunk cabbage. Suddenly, about a hundred yards in front of our truck, a small black bear darts out of the woods near a muskeg and rushes across the road. We slow down next to the bull pines where the bear had emerged. My dad points to the skunk cabbage nearby. He says that because skunk cabbage grows in wet, muddy areas, you can often see a bear's footprints near it. It works like a warning system for us about bears being in the area.

Take notice of the bear's huge paw prints pressed
into the muck. Take notice of the trampled green leaves,
of the deep holes where the roots once were.

Traditionally, the Tlingit used the skunk cabbage's water-repellant leaves like wax paper for lining baskets. Locals still use the leaves for lining ovens dug in the ground or sand, and for wrapping fish for steaming. When folded, the leaves can form drinking cups or berry-picking baskets. When spread out, they make a food-prep space. Dried and ground leaves were traditionally used for thickening foods, since the drying and cooking process breaks down the calcium oxalate, making the leaves edible.

Inhale the warm earth, the scent of new growth,
the mossy muskeg. Good medicine for the mind and spirit.

Despite not being suitable for eating by humans in its raw form, skunk cabbage has external medicinal applications. The roots are used to make a poultice for swollen muscles and joints, and for treating burns. People use the leaves to steam in sweat lodges.

When pressed to the skin, heated leaves can draw out splinters and thorns. I've heard people say they have seen wounded bears roll in skunk cabbage leaves to adhere them to their wounds like bandages. The plant's healing properties are reflected in the Tlingit saying "yee yoo x̱'atángi áwé haa sinéix̱ a yáx̱ yatee x'áal' a káx' haa s'éil' x̱'éiyi"—your words are healing like the skunk cabbage applied to our open wounds.

Hundreds and hundreds of flies buzz around the plants.
The spider spins her web nearby.

At Earl West, the end of the road, my dad parks the truck. We eat lunch at a picnic table, and afterward I spy a large patch of skunk cabbage nearby. Small sticks and dead roots from last year's crop are ground cover for the bright, newly bloomed plants. I carefully step around them and then lie down. The ground is warm and wet. The plants surround me, eye level, and with my camera I take photos of the plant's insides, alive with insects. The smell is delirious and exotic. *This wouldn't be a bad place to breathe my last breath,* I think to myself with the warm spring sun shining down, and inhale the scent of skunk cabbage.

Like the deer, I am careful where I tread. I am like the beetles and
the flies drawn to scent, and like the bear I am drawn to wet earth.
Like my father, I am drawn to travel the trails and dirt roads
to search for wonder, to search for spring.

ROASTED SALMON IN SKUNK CABBAGE LEAVES

MAKES 2 SERVINGS

Nothing beats making this outside in a firepit.
Wrapping the salmon in skunk cabbage leaves keeps
the steam in and gives the fish a slightly smoky flavor.

Up to 4 freshly picked large skunk cabbage leaves

2 salmon fillets, about 5 ounces each

1 lemon, or 3 tablespoons lemon juice or Spruce Tip Juice (page 20)

½ cup whole or chopped salmonberries

2 teaspoons chopped spruce tips

Freshly ground black pepper

Garlic powder

Spruce Tip Salt (page 20)

Chopped or sliced onions (optional)

Prepared tartar sauce or berry sauce, for serving

Make a fire in a firepit and let the fire die down to hot coals before putting a grate over it.

Place 2 skunk cabbage leaves on a clean surface. You are going to wrap the salmon in the leaves, so depending on the size of the fillets and the leaves, you may need 2 skunk cabbage leaves to enclose one fillet—overlap a second leaf if needed. Arrange the fillets on top of the cabbage leaves. Squeeze the lemon juice all over the fillets. Top with the salmonberries and chopped spruce tips, dividing evenly, then sprinkle with black pepper, garlic powder, and Spruce Tip Salt to taste.

Wrap the fish in the leaves. Then wrap the salmon-filled leaves in aluminum foil. Place the fillets carefully on the grill grate. (Alternatively, place the wrapped fillets in a cast-iron pan and cover with foil, then set the pan on the grill grate).

Let the fish cook on the grill until the flesh has turned a lighter color and flakes nicely when prodded with a fork, about 30 minutes, depending on how hot the coals are. With hot pads or mitts and a grill spatula, transfer the fish to a baking sheet or platter.

Carefully remove the foil and put the leaf-wrapped fish on a plate for your guest. Let them unwrap the skunk cabbage leaf before digging in. Serve with your favorite tartar or berry sauce.

HARVESTING
THE SOON BLOOM

The children head down the small trail toward the beach.
They're excited because it's spring in Southeast Alaska and that
means popweed harvesting. In our boots and raincoats, my daughter,
my great-niece, my grandchildren, and I make our way through
the boulder patch to the rocky end of the beach. Picnickers don't
typically use this part of the beach, but the starfish, sea anemones,
and popweed harvesters love it.

Sámi and Tlingit values include experiential learning, so today
at the beach I'm teaching the children how to harvest popweed.
Lately I've been referring to popweed as the "soon bloom" because
it might be the earliest spring plant I've harvested. It seems earlier
than other spring indicators, even skunk cabbage and pussy willows.

I stop and survey the beach. It's perfect! There's lots of popweed
growing between high and low watermarks on rocky shorelines.
Harvesting popweed is an activity children and Elders can do,
especially if the beach is easily accessible.

People know *Fucus gardneri*, the bright-orange-and-brown
seaweed draping Southeast Alaska's beaches, by many names:
tayeidí (Lingít), t'ál (Haida), bladderwrack, fucus, yellow seaweed,
rockweed, dead man's fingers, and more. Varieties of bladderwrack
are found throughout Alaska, in the British Isles, Europe, and on
both the West and East Coasts of the United States.

I inhale the cool, salty air. Handing out bags and small buckets to the children, I instruct them: "Don't cut yourself with the scissors. No running with the scissors. And don't stomp all over the seaweed."

They look around and I know it's impossible not to step on a barnacle or a blue mussel or a patch of popweed. "But Mummo, it's everywhere!" says Grandson Jonah.

"Just be respectful," I say. "Now, we have to thank the seaweed for letting us harvest it. Gunalchéesh." They all know the Lingít word and repeat it together.

I bend down to a big popweed-covered boulder and the children gather around. "See, this is when the popweed is first turning yellow," I say. They bend down and inspect the rock. "It's not puffing out yet." I pick a seaweed frond and put it in my mouth. "You can eat it." They each try it. Crunchy and both sweet and salty.

For thousands of years, cultures have used popweed for medicine and food. It's a common herbal supplement and high in antioxidants. There are known properties in popweed that treat thyroid disorders and increase metabolism. It's also used as an anti-inflammatory and for skin irritations. Too much of it can cause loose stools, though, and it can inhibit blood clotting. Studies have linked popweed with higher levels of the good cholesterol, HDL, and improved digestion due to its alginic acid. All I tell the children is, "It's good for you."

I lift up the sides of the popweed bunch, revealing its tough holdfast adhering the seaweed to the rock. I reach my hands along the stem just a couple inches below the bulb and show the children where to cut. We don't take too much from one rock, as we want to leave some for the smaller tidal creatures who use the seaweed for their sheltering place. Instead, we go from rock to rock and harvest here and there. And we never forget to thank the plants.

I find a different bunch of popweed in the next life stage and call the kids over. "Here, this one is just puffing up a bit," I tell them. We taste the new tips, the bladders or air sacs of the seaweed. They're delicious. Then we find popweed in the next stage, where the bladders are starting to puff up, and we eat some. Finally, I pick a large popweed, though most aren't fully bloomed yet. I hold up the bulbous seaweed and move my hand like the ocean waves over the boulder. "These air sacs let the weed float straight up when the tide comes in."

As a kid, I enjoyed the sound of these air sacs popping beneath my feet. For most of my life, I've used the gooey liquid in the air sacs for medicine. I break the sac in half. "See the goop?" I point out. "Your Grandpa Elmer used to put this on his cuts and pimples." The youngest grandchild shows me a tiny scratch on her hand. I rub the seaweed ointment on it. She insists it feels better already.

"Go ahead," I say to the children. These short lessons over, they take off down the beach, each stopping at their own rock to harvest. I watch them for a bit as I consider the children's lineages represented: Frogs, Kittiwakes, Eagles, and Ravens are down on their knees in the wet sand, lifting seaweed from the boulders. Teaching the next generation is an important aspect of managing our fishcamp. I walk down the beach from boulder to boulder, helping the children and filling my own basket.

After about an hour, one grandchild discovers a green starfish and a bullhead. Another decides the snacks we've brought are more interesting than the seaweed. Grandson Jonah and his cousin Rhiannon continue to pick and pick and pick popweed, though. Rhiannon spends most of her time meticulously harvesting a very clean product.

After a snack break, playtime, beach exploration, and more harvesting, it's time to go our separate ways. The kids have had enough, and I'm done too. At home, I experiment with drying the seaweed. My friend Amy O'Neill Houck, a writer and the publisher of *Edible Alaska*, instructs me on how to roast the seaweed, a favorite of hers. I bake the popweed on trays at three hundred degrees for about half an hour. Baking time depends on the oven and how much seaweed is on the tray, so I turn the pans during the roasting and check it often. About midway through, the seaweed magically turns bright green before getting darker. Finally, it is dry and crunchy. The bladders pop in my mouth and it's good. I try Parmesan cheese on one batch, but I like it better plain. I save some fresh popweed to use it in salads for the week while my dad grinds some of the dried popweed for a seasoning. I take baggies of roasted popweed to friends and family. It's a new healthy snack.

There's something exciting when one season changes to another, but especially from winter to spring. Next spring, as the snow melts and the rains come, I'll walk the beaches, bend over the boulders,

Grandson Jonah Hurst harvests popweed from 8-Mile beach.

looking for the soon bloom—the first slight change in color on the tips of the popweed. Then I'll know it's really spring.

HOW TO HARVEST POPWEED

- Find a good beach with as small human population nearby as you can. You'll need scissors and a container like a basket or cloth grocery bag.

- Scan the beach for a rock with a lot of popweed on it. Going at low to mid-tide heading out will give you time to harvest.

- Cut only the small new growth beneath or a couple inches from the tips of the seaweed. Don't pull off the holdfast that sticks the seaweed to the rock. Harvest only a half dozen or so bunches from each rock, then move on to another rock.

- When your bag is filled, you have enough. Don't harvest more than you can eat; if you do, then share with others.

- At home, cut the seaweed tips from the fronds. Leave a bit of stem if you want. Be careful not to pop the bladders, cutting right below them. Basically, you want the bladders with a tiny bit of stem.

POPWEED STAGES & WHEN TO HARVEST

Popweed has a variety of uses at each stage of its life. The following are suggested guidelines because people harvest popweed differently.

STAGE 1: The popweed's tips (bladders or air sacs) lighten in color. Harvest the flat new growth.

STAGE 2: The tips pop out and start to fill—perfect for harvesting. It has a mildly nutty and salty taste at this stage, and you can dry it or eat it fresh.

STAGE 3: New tips! It's mild and salty. Dry the popweed at this stage.

STAGE 4: Bladders are filled and knobby. The inner substance is gooey. Harvest at this stage to make medicines. Some people dry the popweed and make powders for tea or medicines.

STAGE 5: The bladders mature and become large. There's good medicine inside.

OVEN-DRIED POPWEED

MAKES 1 QUART

*What's a better snack than popcorn while you're
watching a movie? Popweed! What's better than
potato chips when you're craving a crunch snack?
Popweed! Called bladderwrack, rockweed, yellow
seaweed, or tayéidi in Tlingit, popweed can be eaten
fresh or dried, but it lasts longer when dried.*

Canola oil (optional)

1 gallon popweed, rinsed in
seawater and cleaned of
barnacles or snails

Finely chopped spruce tips
(optional)

Freshly grated Parmesan cheese
(optional)

Preheat the oven to 300°F and lightly oil 4 baking sheets or line them
with parchment paper. Spread out the popweed in a single layer on
the sheet. If desired, sprinkle finely chopped spruce tips or Parmesan
over the popweed, but be careful not to over-season it, as the cheese
will contribute salt and seaweed is already naturally salty.

Put the baking sheets in the oven and bake. The popweed will turn
bright green as it heats before it starts to dry out. Check for dryness
every 20 minutes, rotating the pans on the rack as necessary. After
45 minutes or so, take the seaweed out and check for dryness and
crunch—it should darken in color. If it's not done yet, put it back in
the oven for about 10 minutes and test again.

Store the dried popweed in Mason jars or sealable plastic bags.

CEREMONY

I am with my husband and our four children in an aluminum skiff near an island. We are towing one end of a long rope with a large hemlock branch tied to it. We are looking for the best place to set a green-needled hemlock tree branch out in the water to collect herring roe. Using a long rope, we tie off the branch to a larger tree on the shoreline. We'll leave the branch to bob and sway in the water, letting the tide flow in and out and hopefully enticing herring to lay their eggs on the branch's thin, green needles. This is the same technique that my husband's and my children's Tlingit ancestors have used for thousands of years.

While the tree soaks in the water and eggs accumulate, my children and I walk the beaches on the small island, pulling herring eggs off the rocks and eating them. The tide has left them as gifts. I put some eggs into my youngest daughter's mouth. She chews them and smiles at me. Around us, flocks of shorebirds and eagles share in the harvest. Some of these gull types are my children's Clan family: the black-legged kittiwake is one of their Clan crests. We walk the forest edge and I place my hand on an old spruce tree.

"Feel the bark," I say to my oldest daughter. She touches it then leans in close to sniff it. Next, I walk over to a hemlock tree. "Now, feel this one."

She rubs her fingers across its bark. This daughter, my oldest

Holding herring eggs on hemlock branch.

child, is the one I've chosen to remember our stories, so I tell her a story about how Beaver and Porcupine were friends. One day, Porcupine invited Beaver to his house. A bear frightened them both up a hemlock tree. When the coast was clear, Beaver climbed down, leaving long striations in the tree's bark with his claws.

"You can recognize hemlock bark because of its long striations going down the length of the tree," I tell my daughter. "These are the marks left by Beaver." We are participating in the ceremony of man and nature, of story and family. The old stories carry Traditional Knowledge.

After a picnic lunch on the beach, we climb back into the skiff and head to where the hemlock branch is soaking. We haul it into the skiff, heaving it over the gunwale. Thick herring roe dangles from the branches. Our Elders view the herring roe as a sign of life's continuum. In the spring, after the herring have spawned in the Sitka region, their eggs are distributed to the smaller villages like Hoonah and other communities in Southeast Alaska. Much of the roe is saved for memorial parties in the fall. Before we take our share home, we distribute herring eggs to relatives and friends.

At home, we treat ourselves to herring eggs blanched in boiling water. The eggs remain on the branch's needles, but we pick the eggs off. We sit around our table. A large bowl brims with eggs. I've made a salad with the last package of beach greens I'd put up for the winter: goose tongue and beach asparagus. We eat herring eggs with soy sauce or with bits of black seaweed sprinkled on top. We dip them in seal grease and the grease drips off our chins. We tell the story of our day, creating new stories. We recall the chop on gray water, the pungent smell of roe, the deafening sound of hungry gulls, and the Elder's face when she opened the door to find my youngest handing her a bag of herring eggs. This is our ceremony.

CUTE-LITTLE-RAVEN'S HERRING EGG SALAD

MAKES 6 TO 8 SERVINGS

This is my daughter Vivian's recipe. Her Tlingit name Yéilk' means "Cute-Little-Raven." Herring eggs are delicious to eat with melted butter, seal oil (grease), hooligan oil, or soy sauce. This recipe is a great way to use up excess herring eggs. You can add small whole or chopped shrimp to the salad if you like. Make a big bowl to bring to potlucks, or cut the recipe in half for a smaller family.

4 to 5 cups herring eggs, still attached to hemlock branches or seaweed from harvesting

Salt

4 cups shredded or chopped iceberg lettuce

2 cups shredded or chopped red lettuce (or substitute half with romaine lettuce)

2 stalks celery, chopped

1 cup cooked and chopped bacon

½ cup shredded carrots

10 ounces (about 2 cups) fresh shelled English peas, or frozen and thawed

½ cup mayonnaise

¼ teaspoon soy sauce

Freshly ground black pepper

Using garden scissors, trim the herring-egg-laden hemlock branches into manageable lengths, about 8 inches or so long. Keep the branch end long enough so you can easily handle the herring eggs by holding onto the branch, or use tongs. If your herring eggs are on seaweed, then you don't have to trim anything and can use tongs to hold them.

Set a large colander in the sink. Fill a large bowl or pot with cold, salted water and place it in the sink as well.

Bring a large 2-quart pot filled with lightly salted water to a boil on the stove. When the water boils, turn the water off and leave the pot on the burner. Blanch the herring eggs by dipping them into the hot water for about 5 seconds. Push them down with a large wooden spoon if necessary to keep them submerged, but watch the time or you'll overcook them.

Take the blanched herring eggs over to the sink and place them in the colander. Repeat if you have more eggs to blanch. If you don't, then dip the colander filled with herring eggs into the cold salted water bath for a few seconds and then quickly remove. Air-dry the eggs or pat them dry with a paper or cloth towel.

After the herring eggs have cooled, remove the eggs from the branches and clean out any hemlock needles. You'll need about 5 cups of eggs for this recipe. It's okay if there are a few hemlock needles remaining on the eggs.

In a large bowl, combine the blanched herring eggs, lettuce, celery, bacon, carrots, and peas. Add the mayonnaise, soy sauce, and lots of freshly ground black pepper. Mix well, then taste and adjust for seasoning. Serve right away or refrigerate until serving time. This salad will keep for 3 to 4 days in the refrigerator.

EAT YOUR TREES

"Doesn't Mummo know how to cook without spruce tips?"

Grandson Jackson asked his mom, my daughter Brea, this question. She explained that I'm experimenting with spruce tips. It's true: this season I've made spruce tip white chocolate candy, spruce tip truffles, and spruce tip cake donuts with salmonberry glaze.

No wonder Jackson asked.

> *Spruce tip hummus, spruce tip pesto, spruce tip salsa,*
> *spruce tip corn tortillas, spruce tips in salmon tacos,*
> *spruce tip hot crab salad, and spruce tip mayo.*

Grandson Jonah follows me down the trail to the beach, carrying our woven cedar basket. Spruce branches hang low over the logs. I show Jonah which tree is a spruce. I touch the bark, inhale the scent. I tell Jonah to thank the tree and he says, "Gunalchéesh." Every time we move to a new section, we thank the trees by saying, "Gunalchéesh, shéyi." We tell stories while we pick, letting the animals know we're here.

I say, "We are out picking spruce tips, Grandfather." And we remember not to say b-e-a-r out loud in the woods.

> *Spruce tips in macaroni and potato salad, spruce tips in*
> *halibut enchiladas, spruce tips in salmon patties and salmon nuggets,*
> *and spruce tips in halibut patties and crab cakes.*

I point out other types of trees. I've shown my grandchildren how to tell spruce from hemlock. The appearance and texture of spruce bark is like rounded dragon scales, while hemlock is striated with vertical marks from where Beaver dragged his claws down the bark. I instruct them in how to tell the stages of spruce tip ripeness: "Gítgaa, spruce needles. You can tell they're ready. Look at the light green color and look how long they are. See their closed needles. See their open needles."

Spruce tip shortbread, spruce tip teacakes, spruce tip Oreos, spruce tip brownies, spruce tip blueberry jam thumbprint cookies. Spruce tip blueberry muffins, spruce tip cranberry muffins, spruce tip muskeg muffins, spruce tip poppyseed muffins, and spruce tip chocolate cake pops.

At five years old, Jonah's attention span is short and he heads off searching for rocks. I tell him not to keep too many because we have to carry them back. Picking spruce tips is work, but also meditative and fun. We are inviting his cousins Timothy and Jackson to the fishcamp to help package up the spruce tips to give to the Wrangell Cooperative Association, our local Tribal agency, for distribution to local Elders and people with disabilities. I explain to my grandsons that their ancestors are from the Kake and Glacier Bay areas and that we are guests of the Shtax'héen Ḵwáan, the Stikine people of the Tlingit in Wrangell.

Spruce tips with sugar on toast, spruce tips in oatmeal, spruce tip water, spruce tip syrup, spruce tip jelly, and spruce tip huckleberry pancakes. Add to muffins, add to berries with milk, sprinkle finely chopped spruce tips on scrambled eggs, and add to vegetable omelets.

Back at the fishcamp, we set up small tables. Jackson, Timothy, and Jonah help package spruce tips into plastic freezer baggies. Spruce tips tumble to the floor and I scoop them up and rinse them off, setting those aside for our supply. With measuring cups, we scoop out two-cup and four-cup portions.

Spruce tip lemonade, spruce tip blueberry lemonade, spruce tip
salmonberry lemonade, spruce tip thimbleberry lemonade.
Spruce tip iced tea, spruce tip blueberry iced tea,
spruce tip salmonberry iced tea, spruce tip thimbleberry iced tea,
spruce tip red huckleberry iced tea, and spruce tip ice cubes.

"Auntie Viv and I are writing a cookbook," I tell my grandsons. They look up at me, their hands grasped around measuring cups, spruce tips overflowing.

"Are you going to write about spruce tips?" Timothy asks.

"Yes, how did you know?"

He shrugs, "You always talk about spruce tips."

I tell my grandsons about the importance of spruce trees—how eagles nest in the ones in our neighborhoods, how salmon dying in the streams help nourish the spruce trees growing near the streams, how the birds and bears drop salmon guts in the forest, how our relatives and friends make jewelry and baskets with spruce roots. I explain how we get only a short time to harvest spruce tips each year.

Spruce tips in clam chowder, salmon chowder, vegetable soup.
Add to Halibut Olympia, use as seasoning on salmon and rockfish.
Spruce tip salmon rice noodles, spruce tips in spring rolls,
edible spruce tip forks and spoons.

At the Tribal office, Jonah and Jackson each carry in a bag filled with spruce tip packages. Timothy carries a case of assorted jams and jellies. They happily gift these harvest products. We pose for a photo with our spruce tips and make an appointment to show Tribal citizens the best places to harvest around the island in order to pass on spruce tip knowledge, a gift to the next generation. "We won't get scurvy!" Timothy declares in the Tribal office, demonstrating his nutritional knowledge of spruce tips, which are high in vitamin C.

Spruce tip Labrador tea, spruce tip salt and
spruce tip sugar, spruce tip ice cream, and spruce tip beer.

The main question I'm asked by prospective harvesters is: what do spruce tips taste like?

"Like trees," I answer. "A bit tart, like a pickle."

If I go on to describe the recipes I use spruce tips in, I often get funny looks, because who wants a pickle taste in cake donuts? Vivian says spruce tips are like the herb rosemary. Maybe spruce tips are an acquired taste.

Another spruce tip season is done. Now, with my supply in the freezer, I brainstorm recipe ideas: spruce tip and berry teas, spruce tip fireweed scones, spruce tip granola, salmon and spruce tip casserole...

The next day, I stand in the entryway at my daughter Brea's house, holding a plate of freshly made blueberry oatmeal bars. I ask Grandson Jackson, "Guess what's in them?"

"Spruce tips," he says, trying not to smile. "Do you make *everything* with spruce tips?"

I hand him the plate. "Eat your trees."

SPRUCE TIP TIPS

- Spruce tips can be harvested in the spring until the needles spread and they begin to get woody.

- Store whole spruce tips in the freezer in sealable plastic bags for up to a year. When you want to use them, just take them out from the freezer and chop.

- When making spruce tip juice, don't forget to reserve the pulp that's strained out! Freeze the spruce tip juice and spruce tip pulp in separate containers to use later.

- Remember the Rule of Eights: 8 whole spruce tips (or 1 to 2 tablespoons of chopped spruce tips) per recipe if you love the taste; 4 whole spruce tips (or about 1 teaspoon of chopped spruce tips) per recipe if you're not quite sure.

- Spruce tips (raw, pulp, and juice) go well in baked goods, pasta and fish dishes, and drinks.

- Pair spruce tips with other spring or summer edible plants: berries, fireweed, devil's club, fiddleheads, dandelions, seaweed, and goose tongue.

SPRUCE TIP ICED TEA

MAKES 1 GALLON

If there's an occasion to gather with friends or hang out with my community, I bring this iced tea to share. Spruce tip iced tea is at every fishcamp picnic and dinner, and often there's a glass of spruce tip iced tea on my desk when I'm writing. For added flavor and decoration, toss in a few fresh or frozen whole spruce tips, fireweed blossoms, or berries into the jug of tea.

6 cups water

10 to 12 teabags of your choice

¼ to 1 cup sugar or honey

¼ to 1 cup Spruce Tip Juice (page 20)

In a 2-quart pot, bring the water to a boil. Remove from the heat and add the teabags. Press the teabags down with a wooden or plastic spoon. Let the teabags steep for 3 to 4 minutes, but no longer. Squeeze the teabags while removing them from the liquid. Add the sugar or honey. If this is your first time making spruce tip iced tea, start with ¼ cup of sweetener as you can always add more later. Stir until dissolved.

Let the tea cool before transferring to a 1-gallon container. Add the Spruce Tip Juice ¼ cup at a time, to your taste. Fill the rest of the gallon container with water. Adjust the Spruce Tip Juice and more sweetener to taste. Pour into tall glasses with ice and serve.

MY FATHER'S SMOKEHOUSE

K̲aachx̲aana.áak'w, "K̲aachx̲an's Little Lake," is the Tlingit name for Wrangell, Alaska, where my fishcamp is located. In the late 1800s K̲aachx̲an was an Elder who lived in a big, old smokehouse he'd converted into a livable structure near the Inner Harbor area, which resembles a picturesque lake at high tide. Seems like a good idea to me. I love smokehouses. My dad built an outhouse-sized one with five racks and a floor lined with metal for holding a smoky fire.

My grandsons Timothy and Jackson, both in grade school, are visiting the fishcamp for ten days. Today, my dad—their great-grandfather—and I are teaching them to smoke king salmon the way he learned to smoke salmon from his dad. The boys sit at a small table and begin transcribing their great-great-grandfather's smoked salmon recipe. As a way to help them remember, I have each grandchild write the steps for brining and smoking fish. First, thaw the frozen king salmon fillets in a tote overnight. Second, cut the salmon in thick slabs.

Later, on our large prep table outside, my dad and I slice the salmon into manageable pieces. Bald eagles congregate in the trees above. I tell my grandsons they are the Clan opposites of those eagles because they are Ravens, or T'ak̲deintaan. There are two Tlingit moieties, matrilineal half-divisions, to which Tlingits belong: Eagles and Ravens. The eagles screech at us as we prepare the salmon for smoking. A few squirrels skitter up the nearby alder tree. We shoo our dogs away. Everyone is curious.

Afterward, Grandson Timothy fills a tote with water using a garden hose. When the tote is half-filled, my dad opens a box of salt for the grandsons to pour into the water. They take turns pouring the salt and stirring the brine with a stick. Next, Timothy puts a large potato into the brine and it sinks to just below the surface.

"Needs more salt. The potato has to float," my dad says. He pours more salt into the brine and the potato pops up to the surface. "Perfect." As we load the salmon, I repeat the lesson to the kids: use enough salt until a big potato floats.

I think about what our smokehouse means to us and to our family, to the generations to come, and how my children's ancestors' smokehouses were once deemed "illegal." After World War II, the government, acting through the US Forest Service, burned or tore down any "unused" cabins and smokehouses on federal land. Those cabins were not abandoned—they were summer fishcamps. The government considered those families who owned the fishcamps trespassers, despite their having fished there since time immemorial.

For thousands of years, smokehouses were proof of Clan ownership for the Tlingit, proof of a thriving culture that depended on salmon. Often when the first colonizers saw an old smokehouse, they assumed it was abandoned. Throughout the 1930s, '40s, and '50s, the US government destroyed many of the smokehouses and fishcamps in Southeast Alaska. Even recently, my children's relatives had to deal with this.

For us, the smokehouse has always been an important part of our lives. One of my early memories is my father stoking kindling on the smokehouse fire, then bringing smoked salmon inside the house for us kids to try. I remember him giving out his smoked fish in paper sacks to family and friends around town. Smoking salmon is about sharing. Today, I'm grateful I have a smokehouse and I'm able to smoke salmon alongside my dad and share it with my children and grandchildren. I can't imagine how grieved Tlingit families and Clans were—and still are—because the government destroyed their smokehouses. Yes, the Forest Service has since

Salmon soaks in salt brine before being smoked at Mickey's Fishcamp.

apologized, recognizing the devastating impact that the destroying of smokehouses had on Southeast Alaska Native communities, but the damage to language continuity and Traditional Knowledge for subsequent generations has been done.

After brining the salmon, we pour the fish slices from the tote out onto a large screen with a bucket below to catch the water. At each stage of the process, I have my grandsons read the steps on the recipe they've written. "What does it say?" I ask them.

"Glaze the fish for twenty minutes or less," Grandson Timothy reads, "until it's shiny."

Timothy and Jackson help us arrange the fish onto the prepared racks. When a rack is full, my dad loads it into the smokehouse. We repeat this process until all the racks are stacked in the smokehouse. The door is left open so the air circulates and helps set a glaze as the fish drips.

In 2014, the Alaska Native Sisterhood (ANS) requested an investigation into the destruction and burning of smokehouses. They wanted to make sure that destroyed smokehouses were reconstructed and young people—mainly at-risk youth—and Elders be involved in their restoration. I'm not sure if the government has been taking this request seriously, but I do know many of those strong women of the ANS live in Wrangell; they are my cousins, aunties, grandmothers, sisters, and friends. Their lives were directly affected by the destruction of smokehouses. When I consider how our stories and knowledge are interwoven, I see how my fishcamp life is connected to my father's smokehouse.

Timothy and Jackson stand over my dad as he crouches down in front of the smokehouse, arranging wood shavings, kindling, and newspaper to build the fire. The fire burns hot at first, then settles and becomes smoky later. "You don't want to burn the smokehouse down," my dad tells them.

We sit outside near the prep table talking, watching as smoke wafts up into the hemlocks and spruce and across the small road behind the fishcamp. We tend to the fire and to our stories for hours. This is the best part of smoking salmon. We hear stories of my dad's first salmon and many stories of the salmon that got away. We hear lots of commercial fishing stories. I tell my grandsons about the man who lived in a smokehouse near Inner Harbor. They laugh at the idea of living in a smokehouse, because ours is the size of an outhouse. I tell them about the smokehouses that were torn down. My grandsons turn toward ours and I know they're thinking about this.

Hours later, the fish is done and my dad removes the racks from the smokehouse. Safe internal temperature for fish is 145 degrees. My dad knows how to tell if the fish is done, not with a thermometer, but by what the salmon looks like inside and out and how long the smoke and fire have burned. (The smoking time and final step is a secret he forbids me to reveal.) My grandsons help me take the fish off the racks and put them in pans. Inside the house, we each pick our favorite slice. I choose a slice of white king. My grandsons choose red king.

"Good, huh?" my dad asks, holding a slice of salmon on a paper plate.

"I love smoked fish," Grandson Timothy says.

"Smoke fish is my favorite," Grandson Jackson says.

Later, we call relatives to come pick up their share or to coordinate our delivering the fish. We like to smoke a whole smokehouse full without processing any of the fish in jars; it's the "sharing and eating batch," my dad calls it. Otherwise, for jarring smoked salmon we'd smoke it for less time, then put the salmon in Mason jars and pressure cook it.

At the end of the day, I have salmon slime on my pants and my boots. My hoodie sleeves are rolled up and wet and the sleeves sag. My grandsons are in a similar state. After changing into dry clothes, Timothy and Jackson crawl onto their tent cots on our deck next to the sea. My hair and my hoodie reek. It's a good smell, though. I'm so tired that I don't take a shower and collapse into my bed. We all smell like a smoky alder fire and we dream of salmon.

FISHCAMP SALMON SPREAD

MAKES 2 CUPS

*This spread, featuring salmon and goose tongue
(a beach plant), makes a great topping for pilot bread
(Alaskan-style crackers), a dip for vegetables, or a spread for
your favorite crackers. For a spicy salmon dip,
stir in 2 tablespoons diced jalapeños.*

½ (8-ounce) package cream cheese, room temperature

¼ to ½ cup mayonnaise (or to taste)

½ teaspoon freshly ground black pepper

1 teaspoon garlic powder

1 teaspoon onion powder

½ teaspoon paprika

1 tablespoon chopped onion

2 tablespoons chopped goose tongue or fresh chives

2 cups flaked smoked salmon (see note)

In a food processor or bowl, combine the cream cheese and ¼ cup of the mayonnaise. Add the black pepper, garlic powder, onion powder, paprika, chopped onion, and goose tongue or chives. Add the flaked salmon to the mixture and mix well. Add more mayonnaise, if desired, to adjust the consistency of the spread.

Note: If you don't have access to smoked salmon, use 2 cups regular salmon plus 1 teaspoon liquid smoke.

DAD'S SALMON SPREAD

MAKES 2½ CUPS

This spread is my dad's own creation. Spread it on bread or crackers or use it as a dip for raw vegetables. My dad doesn't use liquid smoke because jarred smoked salmon is always on hand, but we created this version for families who've moved out of Alaska and want to make his smoked salmon dip in a pinch.

2 cups flaked smoked salmon, or flaked cooked salmon and 1 teaspoon Liquid Smoke

1 (5-ounce) can tuna, flaked

3 tablespoons sweet pickle relish

2 tablespoons finely chopped yellow onion

½ cup mayonnaise (or more to taste)

Garlic powder and onion powder to taste

Put the smoked salmon in a bowl. Add the tuna and flake together with a fork. Add the sweet relish, chopped onion, mayonnaise, and the garlic and onion powders. Mix well, adding more mayonnaise, if preferred, for more of a diplike texture.

LESSONS FROM
THE DEVIL'S CLUB LADY

An expert on Tlingit traditional foods and medicines, my daughter Vivian Yéilk' says Tlingits don't see a forest of devil's club, or s'áxt', as an obstacle. "We see it as medicine. A forest of devil's club is a journey of perseverance, a lifetime of intimate connections that bring deep knowledge. We learn respect for it over and over again." We're teaching and learning these values with my grandsons today.

It's a beautiful day in Southeast Alaska and we're heading out to harvest devil's club, a large shrub with big maplelike leaves covered in spines on the leaves and stalk. The ideal spot, Devil's Club Alley, is along the dirt road we are driving on. "This is perfect," I say, noting the shade and a pullout. We pile out of two vehicles—me, Auntie Viv, Great-grandpa Mickey, Grandsons Timothy and Jackson, and Oscar the border collie. The forest surrounds us. Thick berry bushes, ferns, and grass grow beneath the trees. And lots of devil's club.

We call Vivian "The Devil's Club Lady," or sometimes "Devil's Club Auntie," because of her knowledge of and experience with the plant and its uses. She says the first step to making s'áxt' medicine is to learn to harvest it. Preparation is important, she tells us. "Step one: getting into the bushes. You should be clothed with fairly impenetrable rain gear, or else be very careful in the forest. Harvesting a plant covered in thousands of thorns takes patience and caution." We are prepared, wearing long-sleeved shirts, long pants, hoodies, and boots.

It's important to teach Grandson Timothy and Grandson Jackson the Tlingit values of patience and caution. I can use those lessons too. I've always wanted to learn to harvest devil's club, but like many of us who've grown up in Southeast Alaska, I'm wary of its thorns. I also want to help teach the next generation in our family what I learn. When my daughter offered to teach us all to harvest devil's club, I said yes. There's so much to learn about s'áxt' that it can take years. Today, she'll harvest the stalks and we'll help with the rest. Another time, we'll learn to make the medicines.

As we walk, Auntie Viv says to her nephews, "You need to apprentice with a knowledgeable harvester for years."

"You?" asks Jackson.

"Yes, but I learned from Harlena, Florence, and Nora. And Ruth, Irene, Janice... and a whole bunch more."

"That's a lot," Timothy says.

Auntie Viv nods. "You can have many teachers. You're learning basketball from different sources."

Great-grandpa Mickey has already spotted a patch of devil's club. We head for the straight stalks.

"That's good," Auntie Viv says as she approaches the spot. She turns toward us. "Before we harvest, we give thanks and let the plant know our good intentions with the medicine we'll make."

We stand still around her and nod while simultaneously listening for any rustling in the bushes, which can mean bears.

"Gunalchéesh," says Auntie Viv.

"Gunalchéesh," we all repeat in unison.

With her big snippers in hand, Auntie Viv heads into thick bushes taller than her head and disappears. The tops of the devil's club begin to wiggle. There's a snap and a chopping sound.

"I'm going to toss one out," she calls. "But don't catch it. It has thorns." A stalk flies out onto the road. She reappears walking up the embankment holding a leafless branch by the end. "Before cutting, it's easiest to scrape a handle first and then take off the leaves."

Timothy and Jackson and I bring the stalks back the short distance to our parking site. We return to the patch together and walk on farther. "Don't take too much from one area," Auntie Viv says. "A good rule is a quarter or less of each plant system, and then move on."

"There's lots of it here," I comment.

Auntie Viv nods. "You'll see plenty of devil's club, but it's a myth the plant can't be overharvested. It's overharvested in Washington and Oregon. And also in Alaska, close to towns like Sitka and Juneau where it's easily accessible."

Great-grandpa and Oscar stop on the side of the road. Timothy sets out a lawn chair for Grandpa to rest in. Auntie Viv reminds her nephews that in the Tlingit culture, it's important to leave easy-access harvesting areas for Elders and children. "If you have a bit more energy and youth, you should harvest farther from the town you live in," she says.

Auntie Viv heads into the bushes again. Soon she tosses out a couple more stalks. "The thorns on the leaves grab everything," she points out, "making it hard to walk in the woods. Sometimes people clean the stalk where they've cut it, and sometimes they'll bring it out for someone else to clean. Either way, it's easier to clean if you cut off the leaves."

Everything she tells us makes sense. She's a good teacher. We walk back to the truck where we unpack our lawn chairs and set out supplies on the tailgate. We each pick a spot in the ankle-high grass near the pullout and set up our chairs slightly away from one another to give everyone some room. Auntie tells us some Tlingit Elders say it's disrespectful to clean devil's club directly on a trail, at a camp, on a picnic table, or at your house because the thorns can get everywhere and are quite painful.

"Now, let's harvest the medicine," Auntie says. We gather around her to make sure we can see all the steps. She holds up a stalk in one hand and a table knife in the other. She braces her foot on the ground, leans down with the back of the knife's edge ready, and runs it against the stalk. "Scrape the thorns and the thin layer of brown bark off with the dull side. Sharp knives remove too much medicine."

Ideally, the thorns and bark will come right off and reveal the bright green layer, the cambium, which will peel off easily. "Now, cut

Vivian Mork Yéilk' instructs her nephew Jackson Pearson on how to remove thorns from devil's club.

a slit down the stalk with the *sharp* side of the table knife," she says. She opens the green cambium at the slit and peels it down, showing us the inner layer beneath. The earthy scent of fresh devil's club surrounds us. "Peel and remove the cambium. This is used to make medicines." She shows us how to be careful, steady, and patient while pulling the cambium around the knots in the stalks.

Timothy and Jackson head back to their chairs with stalks and their knives. They scrape thorns and bark and peel the cambium off. Even Great-grandpa Mickey works on a stalk. I do my part too.

"If the devil's club is cleaned right away after harvesting, this helps people limit their harvest," Auntie Viv says. "Some will think, 'I can get ten stalks and clean them at home,' but they discover by the time they get home the stalks have dried and are too much work. Then those people throw them away and come back to harvest more."

Jackson's eyes widen. You can tell by his face that he realizes this is a waste of devil's club.

After a couple of hours, we have bundles of rolled-up cambium and a bunch of peeled sticks. Auntie Viv says, "Use the sticks to make walking sticks, drumsticks, or art, but make sure you wipe the liquid off the stalk after you scrape and peel it. If you wipe with your hands, the liquid helps keep your hands from aching and also prevents the stalk from discoloring."

We stand back and admire all the rolled layers of s'áxt' cambium. Auntie says, "Now the medicine is ready to make fresh tea, to be used for a face steam, for the sweat lodge, or a bath soak, or to dry to make medicines with later."

We are so tired and ready to be done with the day. Harvesting devil's club is *a lot* of work.

Margaret Atwood wrote that at the end of the day you should smell like dirt. Smelling like devil's club with dirt under your nails is a wonderful thing. For me and for my grandsons, harvesting s'áxt' is the first of many lessons, the first of many scrapes and thorns, the first of many rainy and sunny days and mosquito bites. Good memories, all. Good lessons, all.

BLACK BEAN SALAD WITH DEVIL'S CLUB TIPS

MAKES 4 SERVINGS

This makes a great bean salad, but you can also turn it into a salsa to serve with your favorite seafood tacos. To turn this into a salsa, just add a squeeze of fresh lime and a sprinkle of garlic powder and chopped cilantro. If you are a devil's club or spruce tip connoisseur, you can add more than the recipe calls for. Adjust to your taste.

1 (14-ounce) can corn, drained

1 (14-ounce) can black beans, drained

1 (4-ounce) can green chiles (mild or spicy), drained and chopped

½ cup chopped fresh devil's club tips (see note)

6 fresh or frozen spruce tips, chopped

1 English cucumber, cut into ¼-inch cubes with the skin

1 jalapeño, chopped

1 avocado, chopped

¼ cup chopped yellow onion, green onion, or red onion

In a large glass or metal bowl, mix together the corn, beans, and chiles. Add the devil's club tips, spruce tips, cucumber, jalapeño, avocado, and onion and stir. Serve right away.

Note: Devil's club tips are harvested in the spring from the top of the plant before the tip unfolds. You can freeze, dry, or pickle the tips to preserve them.

THE UNDERSIDE OF LEAVES

I reach my arm out, moving the Indian celery, and step into the salmonberry bushes. Bright orange berries hang above my head. I close my eyes and see words: *Orlando. Shooting. Gay.* I reach to pull the branches down, but my arms feel weak. I let go and inhale. My body aches in response to stress, especially my arms. I pluck a berry and drop it into the bucket, making a hollow sound.

The dense salmonberry thickets provide excellent escape habitats.

The morning's sorrow, outrage, and fear had crammed my Facebook newsfeed. Due to anxiety, I don't have TV and I don't watch the news—even on Facebook—so navigating social media is difficult for me. Finally, I found and read one article. I sucked in my breath. Typically, I would write early in the day, but after I read the article, I couldn't concentrate. Instead, I put on my hoodie and boots and headed out to pick berries.

Everyone get out of Pulse and keep running.

Orlando is a long way from my salmonberry patch in Southeast Alaska, but the hate is insidious and it is everywhere. I consider the hate it took to plan and execute a massacre, how hate is blind to the spectacular biodiversity of all life. Biodiversity is interdependence and is essential to our survival. I pluck a bright berry and hold it up to the sunlight. How can someone not see that? My berry bucket fills while my chest tightens and I consider if I've forgotten my blood pressure meds, but then I realize it's not that.

The deadliest incident of violence against lesbian, gay, bisexual, and transgender people in the history of the United States.

I pick a few more berries. A yellow tour bus passes by on the small highway beside the bushes where I'm hidden from view, its exhaust trails leaving a memory: I'm thirteen years old on a school bus, and the girl in the seat in front of me turns around and says, "You kissed Audrey. Ewwww!" My face reddens. Murmurs rise and fall in the half-filled bus. My arms collapse into my body, my schoolbook tumbles from my hand. "She *told* me," the girl adds. I deny it. Later, I stop seeing my kissing friend. Instead, I spend time with other kissing girls, the secret ones who don't tell.

Salmonberry flowers often appear before or with unfolding and expanding leaves.

Now, I reach for another berry and consider the natural order of salmonberry plants, having both male and female identity, sharing the same plant body. On that bus long ago, I didn't have a name for how I felt or who I was. Instead, I hid these things and was ashamed. I had no one to talk to and I did not know to look to science and nature for answers.

Salmonberry bushes are monoecious, possessing both male and female reproductive organs on the same plant and capable of reproducing both sexually and asexually.

How can we recover from this, create our own healing possibilities? Life layers itself, story upon story: a tragedy in Orlando, solace in the berry bushes. The salmonberry's asexual reproduction is called layering. Basically, the stem touches the

Salmonberries in a red cedar basket sits on the seawall at Mickey's Fishcamp. The basket was woven by Wrangellite Faye Khort.

soil and grows roots. Birds and insects help with salmonberry reproduction too. There is something about layers and making connections, about reaching out, that makes me consider how we're going to restore our lives. It'll take a community to accomplish that, I decide.

We are dealing with something we never imagined.

First, though, I must take care of myself. Take time out, or, rather, time *in* the bushes. Traditional medicine experts say you can chew up salmonberry leaves and spit them out to put on burns to heal them. You can pound the plant's bark to a pulp and place it on an achy tooth or a wound as a painkiller. Boil the bark in seawater to make a medicine that lessens labor pains and cleans wounds and burns. I could use good medicine. This country, my town, could use good medicine.

The salmonberry bush acts as shelter and
protection for various smaller animals.

I am alive. Many are dead. I can't understand, and yet I *can* understand that this day, the same day, can carry both pain and beauty. I am soothed here picking berries, while families across the nation are in anguish. My offerings to the universe, of solace and hope and despair and shame and joy, are the same: they are the berries dropped at my feet for the birds and mice.

If you're alive, raise your hand.

I raise my hands over my head. The bucket's string is heavy on my neck with the nearly full bucket. I consider the dancers and celebrators of love and life at the Pulse nightclub, their families, their friends. I wonder if anyone on our island will organize a vigil for the shooting victims. Probably not.

The shooting could have lasted a whole song.

I consider my friend Audrey's boldness, how she wasn't afraid, even back then, to express love. She might've loved me. It's likely that tonight, somewhere, she will be holding a candle, wax dripping, leaning against her partner's shoulder. What about the secret kissing girls? Are they reaching out for healing? What about me?

Vigils were held around the world.

My vigil began with the body-memory of berry picking, something I've done every summer since I could walk. I lift the leaves beside me; there, in the underside of leaves, half a dozen large red salmonberries bulge with sweetness. Novice berry-pickers often glance at a bush and decide there aren't many berries, so why bother picking? But I know how to look, how to lift the leaves. I know these intimate leafy veins, the hairy undersides, the thorny stalks, the astringent smell, triggering memory after memory as I continue to pick.

As a producer organism, the salmonberry creates its own energy.

Salmonberry bushes, if they're damaged, can heal themselves, sending roots out from the stems, burrowing into the soil in order to sprout other plants. They keep going. They thrive. I reach for a big, ripe salmonberry and instead of putting it in my bucket, I put it in my mouth. It's juicy and sweet. My plant-body is grateful.

The fence has been decorated with vibrantly colored banners.

The first part of June is often called salmonberry days because this is the time when harvesting begins. I plop another berry into my bucket. I pick another and another. I think about the candlelight vigils that are likely to be planned in other cities and towns. The folks in Juneau are participating in Pride Month activities now and I know there will be nothing like that here on Wrangell. All I've done so far is to change my Facebook profile photo to the pink, purple, and blue colors of the bi pride flag and say nothing.

I step carefully through the bushes, heading deeper and deeper into them. The salmonberry is a riparian, living near stream banks, lakeshores, and tidewaters, meaning its roots help prevent soil erosion. If salmonberry bushes near streams are cut down, the dirt their roots once held can slough off into the stream. Removing salmonberry plants can also cause invasive plant species to take hold. Of course our ecosystem's biodiversity is enhanced by thriving salmonberries. I want to hold onto this feeling of connection between plant and body. I have to.

Restoration: salmonberry is a useful shrub in created wetlands because it transplants easily, has good soil-binding qualities once it is established, and is adaptable to eroded or disturbed sites.

In a bulldozed landscape, a small green tendril emerges, lengthens. Then another, and another. A salmonberry bush begins to grow. It has only two blossoms this year and is a couple feet tall. But next year...

A year after the Pulse nightclub shooting in Orlando, something on our island changes. I use the terms "transforming" or "life changing," and some might even say "miracle" to describe what has happened to our island's LGBTQIA community since the summer of 2016. Someone organized a Southeast Alaska LGBTQIA group on Facebook, which eventually became a Wrangell-specific group. Someone moved to town and needed friends. Someone reached out to me. A root reached out and embraced life.

Salmonberry is strongly rhizomatous,
so one needs to watch its growth carefully.

A handful of LGBTQIA people and allies in Wrangell gathered and organized our island's first Pride March. Then on the Fourth of July we rode on the first Pride float my small community had ever seen. We were *Rubus spectabilis*, beautiful salmonberries.

Pulse has served as a place of love and acceptance.

There aren't many salmonberries this year due to last winter's lack of snow, late-coming spring, and torrential summer rains. Basically, we've had a short, rainy growing season. I probably picked only two buckets of salmonberries. But I'm patient; I have hope for next year's season. I have hope for our island community. We call ourselves Community Roots, the first LGBTQIA group of its kind in Wrangell. We are planning a vigil in the fall for all those who've died in the fight for LGBTQIA equal rights and for all those who've died because of who they are. I will be there with a candle. I will be there with my people.

To mark themselves as "safe."

SALMONBERRY SCONES

MAKES 8 SCONES

Salmonberry scones are a perfect treat on our imperfect days. As we dip a scone into hot tea or coffee, we're reminded there's joy in the little things. Optional additions to add to the dough are chopped spruce tips or ½ teaspoon Spruce Tip Juice (page 20). If you're adding the juice, add a little more flour to compensate for the extra liquid.

2 cups all-purpose flour

¼ cup firmly packed
golden brown sugar

1 tablespoon baking powder

¼ cup cold butter, cubed (or
substitute 2 tablespoons
plain yogurt)

1 egg (or substitute 2 tablespoons
mayonnaise)

4 to 6 tablespoons heavy cream
(or substitute milk, yogurt, or
an almond-coconut milk blend)

½ teaspoon vanilla extract

½ to 1 cup slightly thawed frozen
salmonberries, chopped or
whole

1 tablespoon milk

Coarse sugar or chopped spruce
tips

Preheat the oven to 400°F. In a large bowl, mix together the flour, brown sugar, and baking powder. Using a fork or pastry blender, cut in the butter cubes until the flour looks like small crumbles. Stir in the egg, then the heavy cream and vanilla. Fold in the salmonberries, taking care not to overmix the dough.

Turn out the dough on a lightly floured work surface and knead the dough 3 or 4 times. Try not to overhandle the dough—it should still be slightly sticky and soft. Place the dough onto a baking sheet and gently pat it out with your hand into two circles, each about 6 to 8 inches wide and 2 inches thick. Dip a sharp knife into some flour to coat, then cut the dough into 8 wedges while leaving the circle intact. Do not separate the wedges!

Brush the tops of the dough with a bit of milk, and sprinkle with coarse sugar crystals or chopped spruce tips. Bake in the oven until the scones are golden brown, about 15 minutes. Remove the scones from the baking sheet and let cool on a wire rack before serving.

A FAMILY OF CRABBERS

With his orange-gloved hands, my dad pops the shell off the crab, twists the crab in half, pulls the guts out, and then puts the crab halves in the tote beside him. We're processing Dungeness crab at Mickey's Fishcamp. My dad tells me when his mother first came to live in Wrangell, she worked as crab shaker, meaning she cleaned crabs at the local cannery. Crabbing and shaking run in our family.

We bought these Dungeness crabs from my son, Mitch, who's deckhanding for his dad this summer along with my grandsons Owen, age nine, and Chatham, age six. They're working 225 pots around the Wrangell area. Mitch crabs partly for work but mostly to hang out with his dad. Mitch is also teaching my grandkids how to work hard and to show them that being an employee isn't their only option in life.

Mitch is Tlingit and grew up commercial fishing in Wrangell and Sitka. He worked as a civil engineer in Anchorage for the past twelve years, but he retired young and currently lives in Sitka. "Now, I'm a domestic engineer, a homemaker," Mitch says, "and a fisherman, woodworker, landlord, photographer, stock trader, and teacher."

Mitch's dad has been crabbing for decades, and he helped develop the local fishery. Mitch recalls crabbing on our family's boat, the

F/V *Charmer*, when he was young. He often worked for candy and remembers sorting through what seemed like endless crabs.

As I watch my own dad pull off crab shells, I think about all that goes into crabbing. Depending on your permit size, crabbing can take the entire day. It's easy enough to pull one pot, but the number of repetitions—from 150 to 300-plus—can wear on a body.

Every crabber has a different process, but day-trip crabbers are typically on the water by 6 a.m. Crabbing requires lots of bait, mainly humpies—pink salmon—or seafood waste from the processors. Larger pieces of meat are cut up to fit in bait bags or put on hooks, and some are ground up for smaller bait jars. Crabbers bait up on the way to the first string of pots. They load up more bait before heading out for the next run or after delivering the crab. Every boat has its own technique, but it always involves getting something stinky into the crab pot.

Mitch says that ideally pots should sit on the ocean floor for a day or two before you pull them. The crabbers head out to the first buoy in the string and the captain chooses the approach requiring the least effort, taking into account the direction of the current. The boat pulls alongside the buoy and the crabbers retrieve it either by hand or by using a long pole with a hook. The slack in the line allows the line to be pulled up by hand to be placed in the sheave line hauler. Then the power winch is turned on and the rope is coiled onto the deck. Depending on the line's length, it takes between five and thirty seconds for the pot to surface, at which point it is heaved onto the rail.

After the pot is aboard, the door bungee is opened and the old bait, if any, is removed. The crabs are then sorted to remove the females and the small and soft crabs, which are all tossed back into the ocean. Keeper crabs must be males, identifiable by a narrow flap on the abdomen (female flaps are wide). Crabs must also be hard-shelled, or they won't have very much meat in them and the processor won't buy them. The keepers are put into totes or large trash cans. As long as the weather is cool, the crabs stay alive all day. People can get sick from eating crabs that have been dead for too long before they're cooked, so crabs can only be sold alive. Large boats that stay out for days at a time use tanks full of circulated or

Mickey Prescott cleans Dungeness crab at Mickey's Fishcamp.

aerated water to keep the crabs alive, but most Wrangell boats are day-trip boats. After the crabs are sorted, new bait is added and the pot is reset again.

Mitch says even though crabbing is mostly repetitious and at times monotonous, sometimes something exciting happens. There can be a pot bulging with a single huge octopus, loads of giant snails, or even a halibut. Crabbers may have to fight big waves and sea lions breaking open pots. River sand can hold pots tight on the bottom and sometimes lines get stuck in the propeller.

After picking a string of pots, the crab boat runs to the next set. Running time between strings is often the time to grab a snack, prep bait, or clean the mess on the deck before it sticks. After all the pots are picked, crabbers run to the processor in town. The boat is cleaned on the way to save time after the crab is sold.

A crab boat usually waits in line in the harbor for twenty to forty-five minutes before it can be unloaded. After tying the boat up to the processor's dock, a bin is brought down into the boat. The crabbers dump their totes and cans full of crabs into the bin and then hoist it back up to the processor. Crab storage areas on the boat and large totes that can't be lifted and dumped into the bin at once must be emptied by hand, crab by crab. The deckhands must move fast because there are often other boats waiting. Mitch explains they can't take their time selecting a safe place for their fingers when grabbing a crab either, so being quick also prevents being caught by an angry claw. After unloading, the paperwork is signed and the crabbers head back to the dock to ready the boat for the next day's run.

One of the difficult things about crabbing is crab pots can become detached from their lines and get lost—then they are "ghost fishing," meaning the lost pots keep on fishing without crabbers to pick and empty them. Ghost fishing is a worldwide problem because crabs, including females and young crabs, and other sea life can get trapped in the lost pots and die there. Because this can impact ocean health and species conservation, there are government regulations specifying that the cord that fastens crab pot doors must be cotton twine or "rot string," which falls apart in a short period. This prevents ghost fishing by allowing the crabs and other creatures caught in lost pots to be able to eventually push their way out.

Crabbers can lose pots for a variety of reasons. Waterways around Wrangell have lots of logs floating down from the Stikine River, and these logs can catch buoys and drag pots into deep water. Pots can also be sanded down so much on the ocean floor they become too heavy and can't be retrieved. During crab season, when Wrangell's shoreline is dotted with colorful buoys, the pots can be so close to one another sometimes their lines may be accidentally cut by props. Inexperienced crabbers can set pots too deep for their line and pots can disappear in big tides and strong currents only to be found again at low tide. And worst of all, pots can be taken by thieves, which does happen in Wrangell. Losing pots by any means digs into a crabber's profits.

Now, as I sit outdoors beside my dad watching the crab cooker boil, I consider how our family is connected to crab—from pulling the pots to processing the crab, to eating them. It's reassuring to know that with my grandsons, Owen and Chatham, a new generation is learning to crab. Tomorrow will be a long day picking crabmeat. But tonight, when I fall asleep, I'll be thinking about what I want to make: crab patties, crab mac salad, cream crab on toast, crab crepes, crab casserole, crab dipped in butter...

ISLAND CRAB CAKES

MAKES 6 CRAB CAKES

These crab cakes are flavored with ingredients from around our Southeast Alaskan islands: goose tongue, spruce tips, and seaweed. Serve with either Spruce Tip Mayonnaise, for a rich and spicy accent, or Wild Alaskan Berry Sauce, if you prefer a sweet contrast.

6 to 8 saltine crackers, or more if mixture is overly wet

3 cups cooked crabmeat

2 green onions, sliced

¼ yellow onion, chopped

1 egg

2 tablespoons chopped spruce tips

Handful of fresh goose tongue or 2 tablespoons dried

1 tablespoon dried red seaweed or sea lettuce

1 teaspoon yellow or Dijon mustard

½ teaspoon garlic powder

½ teaspoon paprika

¼ teaspoon freshly ground black pepper

3 tablespoons mayonnaise, plus more if needed

FOR THE CORNMEAL-FLOUR COATING (optional):

½ cup cornmeal

½ cup all-purpose flour

Coconut oil, avocado oil, or extra-virgin olive oil for frying

In a food processor, combine the saltines, crabmeat, green onions, yellow onion, egg, spruce tips, goose tongue, dried seaweed, mustard, garlic powder, paprika, black pepper, and mayonnaise. Process until well blended. If the mixture needs more stickiness to form into patties, add a bit more mayonnaise. If the mixture seems too wet, add more crushed saltines.

Remove the crab mixture from the food processor and divide it into 6 equal portions. Pat each portion into a 3-inch patty. You can cook this patty as is, but for a crunchier crab cake, roll the patty in the Cornmeal-Flour Coating before frying.

To make the optional Cornmeal-Flour Coating, mix together the cornmeal and flour in a shallow bowl. Gently coat each patty with the cornmeal-flour mixture and shake off the excess.

Heat ¼ cup of the oil in a large, deep-sided frying pan over medium heat. Fry the patties in the hot oil until golden brown, about

3 minutes per side. Transfer the crab cakes to a paper towel-lined plate to drain briefly. Serve warm with Spruce Tip Mayonnaise or Wild Alaskan Berry Sauce.

SPRUCE TIP MAYONNAISE

1 cup mayonnaise

¼ teaspoon Spruce Tip Juice (page 20) (optional)

2 tablespoons finely chopped spruce tips

Pinch of sugar (optional)

Sriracha sauce (optional)

In a small bowl, mix the mayonnaise and Spruce Tip Juice, if using. Stir in the finely chopped spruce tips. Taste and adjust for seasoning. You can add a pinch of sugar, or for a spicier mayo add Sriracha sauce to taste. Makes 1 cup.

WILD ALASKAN BERRY SAUCE

1 cup of your favorite jelly or jam (spruce tip or salmonberry jelly is my favorite)

¼ cup soy sauce

2 tablespoons sesame oil

1 tablespoon firmly packed golden brown sugar

2 to 3 tablespoons cornstarch

2 to 3 tablespoons water

In a small saucepan, combine the jelly, soy sauce, sesame oil, and brown sugar. Cook over low heat, stirring constantly, until blended. In a separate small jar or bowl, mix 2 tablespoons cornstarch with 2 tablespoons water to make a thick paste. Add the cornstarch paste to the saucepan and stir over low to medium heat until the mixture thickens, about 30 seconds. If the sauce is too thin, make another paste with 1 tablespoon of water and 1 tablespoon of cornstarch in a small bowl and add the paste to thicken the sauce. If the sauce is too thick, add a tablespoon or two of hot tap water to loosen it. Let stand for a few minutes before serving. Makes 1 cup.

ART-THINKING AT MICKEY'S FISHCAMP

"Art is everywhere in the forest," my dad says as we travel along the logging roads. With our US Forest Service permit, we are looking for tree burls and photographing the muskeg as it blooms. A few years ago, my father started making walking sticks from bull pine (shore pine) burls. A burl, sometimes called a bur, is a round growth covered in bark and is caused by stress on the tree: an injury, virus, fungus, mold, or insect infestation.

Thinking about art is something new to my dad. My elderly dad has realized he's an artist, or at least he has artistic talent. But what is art? Art is something we make by transforming a physical thing, like a tree growth, or something intangible, like ideas or emotions, into something new and different: a burl on a tree into a walking stick, or words into a poem about skunk cabbage.

I had to convince my dad he was becoming an artist because he thought he didn't have an artistic bone in his body. Despite his claim that he's never looked at life as art, his artistic sense keeps appearing. He painted a salmon on an old canoe paddle, made jewelry from fishing gear, and sanded and stained a burl and attached it to the outside of our fishcamp. That's art!

No one is too old to discover art. We never stop learning. Storytelling, painting, poetry, weaving—all increase the quality of life for our Elders, especially when dealing with the challenges aging brings. Eventually, my dad and I started to look for art in everything wherever we went, allowing our minds to come up with all kinds of ideas. Art has added a new element to our father-daughter relationship. We look at things as artists, we see what we can imagine. There's a face in the tree. That driftwood looks like a dragon.

We go up a steep spur off the main logging road and pass a burl too high for us to reach. We consider using ladders to get it, even shinnying up the tree, then decide against it. Once, we looped a rope around a large burl on a stump, tied it to his truck bumper, and pulled it out of the woods. It will make a good table someday.

I've searched the forest for burls many times, but it didn't occur to me until recently to look at beach logs for them. Now, I stand on the porch of the fishcamp overlooking the ocean. My friend Kersten Christianson is visiting from Sitka. With binoculars we spot a large log with numerous burls on it floating out in the water, but it's way too far out even to consider getting it. I think about my Sámi ancestors who had the ability to call whales to shore. Kersten, my dad, and I joke about wishing the log toward us.

In the morning I wake up and head outside onto my porch. The tide is low and the birds are singing. Kersten and my dad are already there. As I approach, my dad says, "Did you look down?" I look over the railing, expecting to see a dead seal, maybe. We've had one wash up before. Then I gasp. There, jammed against the seawall and our stone stairs, is the giant log with burls dotting the sides.

We get the chainsaw and start cutting it before the tide comes back in. How did that log float up to our beach right up to the stairs? Hadn't we seen it float southward past our fishcamp? Of the hundreds of places it could've washed up, it settled on our beach. Maybe my dad called it to shore?

I smile at Kersten. She's an artist and writer whose work is quite magical. Her wishes must've helped too.

Making art requires ingenuity and problem solving. A few weeks later, my dad and I are watching another burl-loaded log float by the fishcamp. Near sunset, the tide brings the log fairly close. My dad says, "I can get that." He puts on his waders, grabs his fishing

Mickey Prescott pulls a log in from the sea for its burls.

pole, and heads down to the beach. He wades out into the ocean and casts again and again, trying to snag the log which seems just out of reach. It's too deep to wade out any further. Finally, he snags it and starts to pull, slowly bringing the log into shallower water. The sun is setting and we need to get the log onto the beach and tied up before it gets dark. My dad starts to tire, so we sit on the rocks waiting for the tide to move the huge log closer, while also pulling the log toward us without breaking the fishing line.

Art activities engage Elders both socially and creatively and stave off loneliness and depression and improve moral and physical dexterity. So does sitting on a seawall and contemplating life. The sky darkens and the sunset is a brilliant orange and I say to my dad, "Well, did you ever imagine we'd be living at a fishcamp, fishing for logs while enjoying a beautiful sunset?"

We finally get the log close enough. My dad wades out and attaches one end of a tie-up line around the log, then wraps the other end around a large boulder atop the seawall. Now secured, the log will wait for us there until morning. Sure enough, the log is still there when we check the next day and we set to work to cut off the burls. One looks like a volcano. Another looks like an old man's face.

Participating in art events and activities improves mood and confidence in our Elders and creates better family relationships. Art has made its way into our fishcamp and is now a big part of our lives. People are living longer, meaning the older population in the United States is growing. Maybe I'll live longer because I trudge through forests and muskeg, and along beaches.

Encouraging creativity and skills in a social environment positively affects psychological, physical, and emotional health. Creativity in an outdoor setting can further boost those effects. As we drive along on another day, we scan the muskeg for gnarly burled limbs. "There," I say, pointing. "I see one." My dad pulls the truck over, and with our boots on and armed with a small handsaw, we head out to inspect the tree.

I'm not sure if searching for material for art projects benefits my dad more than me. Maybe someday I'll be an Elder taking a great-grandchild out into the forest to search for burls. Maybe at that moment, I'll think of this moment—of my dad, of the perfect burl, the smell of moss, and the little white flowers on the muskeg tea blooming around us. I'm sure I'll be walking in the muskeg or along the old logging road using a burled walking stick.

SALMONBERRY–SPRUCE TIP ARTISAN BUTTER

MAKES 2 STICKS

This is like eating jam with your butter. Fresh summer berries are always the best to use, but you can also get out your frozen salmonberries and make homemade butter to brighten a winter day. Use this flavored butter as a spread for crackers, toast, pancakes, or bagels. You can also turn it into a whipped butter spread by beating the butter at room temperature with an electric mixer and adding ¼ cup of powdered sugar or honey to taste. Both the artisan butter and the sweet spread go great on fry bread or homemade biscuits.

3 cups cold heavy cream

5 tablespoons ice-cold water

1 teaspoon salt

1 to 2 teaspoons chopped spruce tips

¼ to ½ cup salmonberries, chopped

Pour the cold heavy cream into a food processor and process on high speed. After about 2 minutes of processing, you'll see the mixture start to thicken, but keep processing until you see clumpy solids and liquid (the buttermilk) in the work bowl, about 4 to 5 minutes. While the machine is running, pour in the ice-cold water. You should see the cream separate more. Pour off the buttermilk into a jar.

Scoop the butter onto a large piece of cheesecloth. With clean hands, squeeze the butter until there's no more liquid in it. Reserve the liquid in the jar with the rest of the buttermilk and save it for other recipes, like pancakes or biscuits.

Place the butter in a bowl and, using a spoon, mix in the salt, chopped spruce tips, and chopped salmonberries. Form the butter into two logs. (Alternatively, you can put the butter onto a cheesecloth and sprinkle the additions on the top, then fold up the cheesecloth in your hands and gently work in the additions as you shape it into a log. Divide the butter into smaller logs.)

Put the butter in your favorite butter bowl and refrigerate. You can keep your artisan butter in the fridge for up to 6 weeks.

BEING MUMMO: FORAGING FOR GOOSE TONGUE

I crouch down on the beach beside my toddler-age grandson Jonah. A field of green clumps of the grasslike goose tongue surrounds us. I tell him, "We call this plant suḵtéitl'." I pinch the end of the word, making a sharp sound, and Jonah mimics me. I explain to Jonah how, before picking it, we first have to thank the plant for giving its life to us. "We have to say gunalchéesh, gunalchéesh."

Grandson Jonah is an important part of our fishcamp. He is one of the reasons why we live here in Wrangell, to teach the younger generation how and what to harvest from the forest, the beach, and the sea. To him, I'm Mummo, which means "grandmother" in Finnish. Being Mummo means it's up to me to keep track of where, what, and when to harvest, and it means passing down knowledge. Being Mummo means sharing.

The favorite goose tongue area Jonah and I are in is located near what once was an early Tlingit village. I wonder how many hands have foraged here over the centuries. Jonah and I pick the tender leaves at the base of the goose tongue, being careful not to pull it out by the roots. With his small hands, Jonah plucks a piece. "Gunalchéesh," he says.

Goose tongue has many medicinal properties. It's a natural painkiller, and is anti-inflammatory, antiviral, and antihistamine. If you're picnicking on the beach and get a mosquito bite, you can pluck a blade of goose tongue and rub the juice on the bite to stop the itching.

Plantago maritima is the scientific name for goose tongue, but I don't teach Jonah those words, mainly because I usually have to look them up myself. I like saying the Lingít names, how the letters feel in my mouth. Grandson Jonah is Tlingit, Alutiiq, and Potawatomi. I love connecting him to the food and traditions of his heritage. As Jonah and I harvest, we say, "Gunalchéesh, suḵtéitl', gunalchéesh, suḵtéitl'," meaning "Thank you, goose tongue."

Jonah holds up a goose tongue leaf. "Eat it," I tell him. "Take a bite." He bites and chews it. He doesn't make a face. "See," I say, "it tastes like a pickle and kind of like the ocean." He takes another bite and then offers me a bite from the same piece.

Most of what I teach Jonah comes from what I learned from my daughter. Vivian studied for years the medicinal and edible properties of Alaska's plants. She tells me some people don't harvest goose tongue after the flowers bloom because the plant can become bitter and less tender as it ages. I go by actual taste: if goose tongue tastes salty and tart, then I use it. I've discovered its taste and texture is dependent upon the weather. One summer the ocean was really warm and the goose tongue hardly had any salty taste and firmed up sooner than usual.

I show Jonah how to gather only a few blades from each plant. I show him the difference between arrowgrass and goose tongue. Arrowgrass, a poisonous plant, resembles goose tongue, but once you know the difference it's easy to tell them apart. Sometimes the plants grow in the same area, so it's important to know the difference. Goose tongue blades are flatter and have ribs, while arrowgrass looks more like a grass and is rounded in shape.

Jonah's attention span lasts a few minutes and soon he's wandering off, stomping in the tide pools, while I finish filling the basket. I always bring my favorite handwoven cedar basket—made by Wrangell artist Faye Khort—with me on foraging expeditions.

Back at the fishcamp, I lightly rinse our harvest in a colander. Jonah helps me spread the goose tongue on baking sheets and place them on small tables near the windows. It's been a rainy year, so we're drying everything inside. I've used a food dehydrator before, but it's easiest to use a baking sheet and dry the goose tongue in natural

Keeping harvesting traditions going, Grandsons Chatham and Owen Mork
learn how to harvest goose tongue.

sunlight (or rainlight). Once the goose tongue is dried, I will crumble
or chop it and then put it in small, labeled baggies for later use.

We use goose tongue year round as a seasoning. When it's fresh,
we use it to make a fabulous ranch dressing, or we steam it or sauté
it with other vegetables. I also pair it with spruce tips in numerous
recipes. Some people have told me they blanch the goose tongue first
and then vacuum-seal and freeze it. I'm going to try that this year.
I have tried freezing it in baggies, but I've noticed when it thaws it
becomes soggy.

Today we are making Wrangell ranch dressing. Beside me, Jonah
stands on a stool at the counter, stirring the ingredients together with
a spoon while I hold the bowl. I say to Grandson Jonah, "Don't you
love the fishcamp? We get to go out and get our own food." I watch as
the telltale greens are slowly mixed into the dressing. Spring is my
favorite time to watch and wait for the goose tongue to start to sprout.
Part of the fun is taking Jonah with me to check for progress. Is it
growing yet? Is it long enough yet? Does it taste ready yet?

As I pour the dressing into the Mason jar, I smile, thinking of the day's foraging adventure. "Mummo, over here!" Jonah had said to me at one point. I turned in his direction, thinking he'd found a great patch of goose tongue. Instead, he was holding a piece of driftwood over his head, as if it were a set of antlers. "Look, Mummo, I'm a deer."

"You sure are!"

Yes, indeed, you are!

WRANGELL RANCH DRESSING

MAKES 16 OUNCES OR 1 MASON JAR FULL

Gather the kids and forage the new growth of sea chickweed, goose tongue, and beach lovage from the beaches around Southeast Alaska, then use the spoils for this savory dressing. Kids love ranch dressing, and this recipe will get them to eat their vegetables, especially if they help forage. This also works as a dip for fish or shrimp.

¼ cup beach lovage (or substitute parsley)

2 to 4 tablespoons chopped fresh goose tongue

2 tablespoons chopped fresh spruce tips (or substitute dried or frozen spruce tips)

1 clove garlic

1 tablespoon chopped fresh chives or green onions

1 tablespoon chopped fresh sea chickweed

1 teaspoon dried goose tongue

¼ teaspoon freshly ground black pepper, or a few finely chopped black peppercorns

½ teaspoon Spruce Tip Salt (page 20) or sea salt

½ cup mayonnaise

½ cup plain Greek yogurt

½ cup coconut milk (or substitute almond or cashew milk)

1 teaspoon Spruce Tip Juice (page 20)

½ teaspoon white vinegar

Using a large knife or food processor, finely chop the beach lovage, goose tongue, spruce tips, garlic, chives or green onions, and sea chickweed, then transfer to a large bowl. Stir in the dried goose tongue, black pepper, and salt.

In a separate bowl, combine the mayonnaise, Greek yogurt, coconut milk, Spruce Tip Juice, and white vinegar. Slowly add the liquid ingredients to the beach lovage mixture, stirring between additions. Pour the dressing into a small jar with a lid and store in the refrigerator for up to 1 week.

13 WAYS OF LOOKING AT DOG SALMON

1. *Téel', dog salmon, chum salmon,* Oncorhynchus keta, *calico salmon, keta salmon, silverbrite, fall salmon, autumn salmon.*
Revered for their eggs. The longest-migrating salmon. The shapeshifting salmon. The drag-show salmon. The salmon with bear scars. The salmon wearing a woven cedar robe. The salmon who fights for life. The chief of all salmon. The sustaining salmon. The adaptable salmon.

2. *Ocean-fresh dog salmon are metallic green-blue on the top with fine black speckles.*
Spawning male dog salmon develop the characteristic Pacific salmon hooked snout and large teeth. Males turn olive-green with what some call "tiger stripes." Female spawners have a dark horizontal band along their sides, and their green color and purple-red bars are paler than those of the males.

Like an alien creature from a movie or new camo technology, spawning dog salmon can shift their colors in seconds, depending on the salmon's mood. And the smaller male dog salmon can shapeshift into female colors to avoid competition and fighting with larger male salmon. These males join the female gatherings, acting and looking like females, mingling and waiting until the right time, hoping to fertilize eggs.

3. *Dog salmon are less oily than king salmon or sockeye. The flesh is lighter in color and has a milder flavor.*

I grew up in a fishing community believing dog salmon was undesirable, but they are a historically important food source for interior and coastal Alaska Natives. Dog salmon make the best dried fish because of their low oil content. They are also great for grilling and smoking.

4. *Dog salmon have the widest distribution of any Pacific salmon. They are eaten by people in Korea, Japan, the Okhotsk Sea, the Bering Sea, British Columbia, and in the United States from San Diego, California, to Alaska.*

The Dog Salmon People are our neighbors, friends, and family— Prince of Wales Coast Town Tribe, Takjik'aan Ḵwáan: L'eeneidí, Téel' Hít (Dog Salmon House), Téel' Yádi Hít (Small Dog Salmon House); Auke Bay Small Lake Tribe, Aak'w Ḵwáan: L'eeneidí, Téel' Hít (Dog Salmon House).

5. *Ocean-bright dog salmon are hard to distinguish from sockeye and coho without looking closely at the gills, fin, and scales. The primary visual identifiers for dog salmon are fewer, shorter, and heavier gill rakers, large eyes, narrow tail bases, and deeply forked tail fins.*

Sitting on our fishcamp porch watching the ocean, my dad tells me how to identify a dog salmon: They do a lot of swimming. They fin the surface. They are lazy jumpers; they don't jump all the way out of the water. The fishermen (seiners) call them "diving dogs" because of the way they dive to escape the purse, or net.

This is important information because my dad has gifted me a subsistence net for my birthday. The net was custom-made by Wrangell Elder Dan Nore.

6. *Dog salmon usually range in weight from seven to eighteen pounds, and measure between twenty-four and thirty-two inches long. The largest recorded dog salmon, caught in British Columbia, was forty-two pounds and forty-four inches long.*

Read what we call "The Directions," a sport fishing regulations booklet. Get a resident fishing license. Get a subsistence permit from the Alaska Department of Fish and Game (ADF&G) or a personal-use permit (free). Go online and print further directions. Keep track of where you fished and what you fished and how many you caught—make sure you take a pen with you. You are allowed fifty pounds of dog salmon in your possession at one time, with no annual limit. You can fish all streams except sockeye streams. No streams flowing across road systems. Call the local ADF&G. Ask questions. Every answer leads to another question. Go down to the local ADF&G office to ask more questions. Know definitions: customary, traditional, resident, rural area, subsistence use, personal use, possession, vessel, domicile, take, one permit per household...

7. *Juvenile dog salmon eat zooplankton and insects, small adult fish, squid, and even comb jellies.*
"You have to be a Philadelphia lawyer to understand the fishing laws of the Alaska Department of Fish and Game," my dad says.

8. *Dog salmon fry do not stay in the rivers. They migrate soon after hatching to the estuaries and ocean, in contrast to most other Pacific salmon species.*
Dad tells me this story: "I walked up Pats Crick Valley hunting for deer. I was in the muskeg when I heard some splashing, so I went over and checked out the creek. It was about three feet wide and beneath the bank I could see some fish. I reached down and pulled up a fish by the tail and it was a dog. What the heck? I put him back. You wouldn't think that one'd be so far inland. It was a mile or two upstream."

9. *Female dog salmon can lay up to four thousand eggs in her lifetime.*
I hold a skein of brined salmon eggs in my hands and gently rub it over the screen, manipulating each bright orange egg into the bowl. It is an intimate and delicate process. I try the eggs: oceany with a hint of soy sauce. At the end of the day, my hands smell like dog salmon eggs. It's a good smell. Grandson Timothy and I take some jars of ikura shoyu (soy sauce–marinated salmon eggs) to the Wrangell Cooperative Association to distribute to our Elders.

Dog salmon ikura in jars.

10. *Dog salmon patties, dog salmon enchiladas, dog salmon with their eggs on rice, dog salmon mac 'n' cheese, dog salmon and their eggs in spring rolls, dog salmon eggs in salads.*

My friend Owen James can fillet a dog salmon in thirty-six seconds.

11. *Dog salmon spawn in the lower reaches of large rivers and coastal streams and often the same rivers as cohos, although cohos spawn further upstream. In the Yukon River there are summer chum and fall chum.*

We set the net and catch fifteen dog salmon, some huge thirty-pounders. We clean salmon on our fish-cleaning table into the night. My daughter Nikka helps package the fish for freezing until we can get to the smoking later in the summer. Our smokehouse is ready and waiting.

12. *In the Pacific Northwest, the dog salmon is the last species to enter fresh water and begin spawning.*

Dog salmon fill up the tote. They've come a long way to get to my fish-cleaning table. Dog salmon are known to migrate two thousand miles up the Yukon River. I consider the long journeys we sometimes make. The dog salmon house screen from Taẋ'jik Aan (Tuxekan) that had once been on the exterior of the Teeyeeneidí Clan house was repatriated and returned to Klawock.

I consider my ancestors, the Sámi, migrating from one season to another, from one landscape to another: sea to forest to tundra. "You bring your home with you" is a common Sámi saying. Better to be on a journey than staying put in one place. We are home because we are *present* in the landscape, wherever that may be. We eat from the landscape. We pick berries. We catch fish. We fillet dog salmon. We dine on flesh and eggs. We make soup from fish bones. I reach into the tote and grab a dog salmon by its gills and place it on the fish-cleaning table. I pick up the knife beside me. I thank the fish—Giitu, gunalchéesh—and begin.

13. *The oldest salmon fossil ever found is fifty million years old, give or take a few years.*
We've been eating salmon for a long, long time.

FISHCAMP IKURA (SALMON CAVIAR)

MAKES 12 SMALL (4-OUNCE) JARS

Dog salmon eggs have a mild, salty sea flavor. Serve these on pilot bread crackers or other favorite crackers. Sprinkle the eggs on your salmon patties, ramen, and rice, or use in spring rolls and salads. Fishcamp Ikura is a great topping on Smoked Octopus Salad (page 119). The brine is versatile and easy to adapt. Try adding lemon zest, tamari, mirin, sake, or spices of your choice.

3 quarts water
½ cup soy sauce
½ cup firmly packed golden
    brown sugar

½ cup salt
3 to 4 skeins dog salmon eggs

Prepare your canning jars first by sterilizing the jars, lids, and rings. Wash everything in hot, soapy water, and then boil the jars for at least 10 minutes and leave them in simmering water until they're ready to use.

In a large bowl, combine the water, soy sauce, brown sugar, and salt to make a brine. Use a wooden spoon (not metal) to mix until the brown sugar is dissolved. If you want to throw in any other additions, now's the time. Mix until the brown sugar and salt are dissolved. Set aside.

Rinse the salmon eggs gently, then separate the eggs from the membrane. There are two methods for doing this.

Mesh method: Place a ¼-inch mesh screen over a glass (not metal) bowl. Put a skein of eggs on the middle of the screen. Turn the skein so the membrane side is up and egg side down, then move the egg sack gently back and forth over the mesh. The eggs should drop down into the bowl while the membrane remains on the mesh. If any membrane gets through to the eggs in the bowl, just pick it out.

Colander method: Fill a glass (not metal) bowl with lukewarm water and leave it in the sink. Make sure your water is not too hot by placing your finger in the water. You should not feel any coolness or heat. Put the egg skeins in a colander, then insert the colander into the bowl. The warm water will shrink the membrane, making the salmon eggs easier to remove. Don't worry if the eggs turn slightly white; when they cool down, they'll turn translucent again. Gently loosen the eggs from the sack with your fingers. Rinse the eggs carefully so the eggs do not pop or squish. Pick out any skein sack material and discard.

Put the loose eggs in a clean colander and lower the colander into the brine until the eggs are submerged. Brine the eggs until they are firm and pop under slight pressure, 15 to 30 minutes. They should be slightly salty with the taste of the sea. Then immediately remove the colander and the eggs from the brine.

Remove the pot of simmering jars and lids from the stove and set aside to cool for about 15 minutes. Drain the water and set the jars and lids on a clean work area. Let jars drip dry upside down or dry with a clean cloth. Spoon the brined eggs into the small glass jars and tightly seal lids and rings on top. Refrigerate for up to 2 weeks.

AFLOAT

My dad and I sit on the porch at the fishcamp, watching the gulls and seals, looking for whale spouts. I take photos, and as I upload them to my Facebook page, I see a local friend's post: *killer whales in front of town by the city dock.* I excuse myself, jump in my car, and head to town. By the time I get there, I've missed them. They're heading to the Stikine River, likely toward the sea lion haul-out on Lesnoi Island.

> *Date: July 26, 2018*
> *Media Release: For immediate release*
> *Center for Whale Research*
> *Subject: Newborn Orca dies.*

In Southeast Alaska we've seen killer whales (kéet) dive under our boat, check us out, and steal our fish. We've seen pods pass in front of town. We know people with Killer Whale Clan crests—they are our family and friends. In 2018, we even welcomed home the Kéet S'aaxw (Killer Whale Crest Hat) to the Dakl'aweidi Clan. We live among killer whales, which is why when many of us Southeast Alaskans saw the news about Tahlequah and her dead calf, we grieved. Tahlequah, also known as J35, is a killer whale from the Southern Resident killer whale population in the Pacific Northwest. She kept her dead calf afloat for seventeen days.

Transients are our visitors. Residents are our neighbors.
Residents are one ecotype of killer whale (orca) that eat mostly
salmon. The other ecotype, transients, eat squid and marine
mammals like seals and sea lions.

I read that seventeen days was a long time for a killer whale to carry a dead infant, but I would've carried my tiny nephew, the one born dying with an underdeveloped brain, for seventeen days. Seventeen days would not have been too long to hold him and to hold vigil.

Like humans, killer whales live in groups. Their lifespans are like ours.
Killer whales, especially resident pods, also have social structures
similar to matrilineal human cultures including the Tlingit.

Humans imagine we are the only ones who are capable of grief and the rituals that accompany it. Sea lion and dolphin mothers grieve over the deaths of their young. Graylag geese, gorillas, chimpanzees, giraffes, elephants, and Western scrub-jays all exhibit grief. Some even conduct death ceremonies.

Just after the calf's death, a half dozen female killer whales swam
in a close circle near Tahlequah and her baby for two hours.

When Tahlequah carried her dead calf around on her forehead, pushing her baby through the sea, we knew. We've felt it too. I've written poems for families of dead children. I've comforted a daughter and friends who've miscarried. My grandma, Nana, as a young wife and mother, lost her young child. Shortly after, she divorced and headed for Alaska to work in Wrangell's canneries. My childhood friend's daughter was hit by a car and killed on the main street in Wrangell, and my young great-niece recently died here in a car accident. A best friend lost two babies, from two different pregnancies, both at term. I wept with her on their graves. A neighbor lost her baby after only four months of gestation. Some friends could not understand why she'd gone through naming the child and then having a funeral—after all, the baby wasn't even to term yet. I understand. A killer whale would also understand.

The killer whale grandmothers—a pod's female leaders—reach
a form of menopause in their forties and can live into their eighties.
Females grow up to twenty-seven feet and can weigh up to
four tons. Grandfathers can live into their mid-seventies,
grow up to thirty-one feet, and weigh eight tons.

Some scientists say Tahlequah exhibited a refusal to accept death—after all, she had carried her dead calf for *one thousand miles*. But it wasn't like she didn't know what death was because she saw death all around her. Sea lion mothers have been known to wail when a killer whale eats one of their babies.

Sometimes our societies, cultures, and families try to dictate our personal grieving timeframe for us, though mourning ceremonies vary from culture to culture and species to species. It's okay to cry out, to keep our loved ones afloat for a time.

As with human cultures, such as the Tlingits with a matrilineal
structure, killer whales form a "house-group" for life—one or
more adult males, several females, and children—with as few
as three members to as many as forty.

In Southeast Alaska we are made up of small island communities. We take care of one another. We celebrate and grieve with one another. It reminds me of a killer whale pod. Killer whales depend on one another to survive. Gathering up in a group, they hold one another up so they can rest. Typically, one whale acts as a lookout.

Once, when I thought my toddler son was dying, as he was seizing again and again, the world sucked me in like a silty river whirlpool and time was warped just like you see in the movies. My wails could be heard far up the Stikine River, I'm sure. He didn't die, but I suffered from nightmares for a few years as my mind tried to make sense of my child nearly dying.

Like humans, larger killer whale pods form from smaller ones
gathering temporarily for seasonal activities like hunting,
looking for a mate, or just being social.

There are times when we can save a baby or a child, when the air moves back into them, when they come back to us cured, stitched up, happy. I've breathed for my son. I once helped rescue a severely abused niece and gave her a second chance at life. Metaphorically, I held her up to the air and told her it was okay to breathe again. She was adopted by a family and grew up healthy.

*At birth, a killer whale calf weighs around
four hundred pounds and is eight feet long.*

By the time my life and your life are done, like Tahlequah we will have traveled a thousand miles with grief and with one another. We bring food, we send cards, we wrap woven and buttoned robes around one another, we dance and pray for one another. We hold forty-day parties, memorials (ḵu.éex'), funerals, wakes, and celebrations of life. Here in Southeast Alaska, there are many things to grieve over and many ways to grieve in this life, but know this: we keep one another afloat. We are not alone. Even crows gather around their dead. Fellow whales circle, holding a dead baby for the mother. Grief is a shared condition.

Flavored waters.

SPRUCE TIP–LABRADOR TEA–SALMONBERRY-INFUSED WATER

MAKES 1 (8-OUNCE) GLASS

Infusing my water with local berries and plants encourages me to drink more water. Also, many of our Elders can't have added sugars, especially in sweetened drinks, so berries provide a healthy alternative.
Be creative and try different combinations of berries and plants to make infused waters. I enjoy clover–spruce tip water, fireweed–Labrador tea water, blueberry water, devil's club bark water, and thimbleberry water.
Adjust the amount of berries for more or less potency.

Whole fresh or frozen spruce tips
Fresh or frozen Labrador tea leaves
Fresh or frozen salmonberries

Water
Honey (optional)

Take your favorite 8-ounce drinking glass (Alaskans use Mason jars) and put in several whole spruce tips, about 10 whole Labrador tea leaves, and a tablespoon or two of salmonberries. Now fill the glass with clean water. Let it steep for a couple of minutes. Add a tiny bit of honey if you want it sweeter. Drink up!

HALIBUT SUSTAINS US

In Wrangell, the fish we eat most often is not salmon but halibut. Halibut is what's in our freezer and on our plates all winter. If packaged correctly, halibut easily lasts a year in the freezer and is probably our most widely gifted fish; it's shared with extended families, brought to potlucks and community dinners, and cooked for fundraisers.

Halibut patties, halibut tacos, deep fried halibut, halibut enchiladas, halibut burgers, halibut nachos, halibut ceviche, halibut lasagna, tempura halibut, halibut fettuccini...

The fish hits the line with a thud and runs with it. I'm using my lucky fishing pole and thick halibut line. I'm in the boat with my dad, my husband, our son, and my sister in our favorite spot. Among my Finnish ancestors in Suomi (Finland), special fishing holes were called the "pits of Ahti," who is the Finnish sea god. This is my secret pit.

The Tlingit artist carved a halibut hook out of a deer bone barb, lashed it with spruce root, fashioned an inner cedar bark leader and a line with a stone sinker, and then finished it with a devilfish design.

I reel the line for a few minutes. The fish tugs and the line heads out again. Meanwhile, everyone on the boat reels in their line to avoid tangling with mine. My pole bends and I let the fish run with it, waiting for it to tire out. "It must be a skate fish," I say to my husband. We've caught several skate fish in this spot, so I am trying not to be too optimistic. Plus, if I declare the fish a halibut, that would be bad luck. I learned from Elders in Hoonah, my children's Clan's home village west of Juneau, not to name the fish or even say we're going out to catch some halibut. I reel the fish in closer to the boat, but it's as if it has seen the hull and realized its fate. It swims down hard, pulling the line out again.

At our fishcamp, halibut fishing is a family event. We take turns heading out to our spots. Sometimes I go, and sometimes I don't get to go. We take our daughters and sons-in-law and grandkids and daughters-in-law and sisters and our brother. Everyone loves halibut. My children's father's family shrimped in the winter and fished halibut and salmon in the summer. I imagine my son's great-grandfather fashioning wooden halibut hooks.

Use a yew branch, stem bent into a V-shape, lashed onto a bone barb using split cedar root, sinew, or bull kelp stem. Bait with octopus. Octopus is the best.

Now we're fishing in only one hundred feet of water because halibut move into the shallows this time of year. The tide changes from outgoing to incoming and the fish bite at the change of tide. I reel in again and soon an apparition appears below the surface. I look over the gunwale at the fish. The larger halibut are female. This one is about sixty pounds or so—it's likely a male. It's a perfect size.

Like snow falling upward, thousands of halibut eggs, hatched in deep water, reach the surface of the sea.

I reel up the fish, keeping its head just beneath the surface of the water so it doesn't jerk its head and spit out the hook. The halibut floats just below the surface, suspended between life and death. Halibut have two eyes on one side of their flat heads. I look down at

Mickey Prescott fillets a halibut on his custom fish-cleaning table.

its beautiful spotted side, like painted camouflage that easily blends with the bottom of the ocean.

Halibut have scales so small they can't be seen.

This fish has given its life for my family. I'm thankful because soon I'll have halibut freshly fried in the pan. Or maybe baked halibut or boiled halibut, útlxi.

Developing halibut float freely for their first six months of life. Baby halibut are carried by the wind and currents to shallow waters.

Because of its size, we make plans to heave the halibut over the gunwales then secure it onboard. I reel the line until the sinker comes out of the water. My son gets the baseball bat in the side compartment on the deck and hands it to my husband. My son's ancestors used to tell the halibut it was being hit with a feather. In Middle English, the word halibut means "holy" (haly) and "flat" (butte). In Lingít, it's called cháatl.

Raven gave all the fish to us as a gift.

I pull the fish over near the side of the boat and its head emerges from the water. Before the fish can thwack its tail and body, my husband says, "Chaa adei yei xat naay.oo" (Please forgive me). He leans over and thumps the fish on the head several times with the baseball bat, stunning it. Then he takes a shark hook—a large hook with a hefty line attached to one end—and pierces the fish in the mouth. Together we heave the fish over the rail and into the boat. If it'd been a larger fish, he would've shot it with a pistol.

As it grows, the young halibut's skull bones bend and shift, a single eye moves over the nose, its mouth moves to the side, the body tips sideways. Recreated. Shapeshifter.

The halibut flops onto the deck and I back up to the cabin door. The fish is still stunned. If it livens up, it may hurt us. The hooks are removed from its mouth and then a line is threaded through the mouth and out the gills, then looped around the tail and cinched into a curve so the fish can't flop. We fasten the line to a cleat and heave the halibut over the side. Once suspended beneath the surface of the water, the halibut's gills are slit and blood slowly pumps out in clouds of life. We take turns saying, "Gunalchéesh, cháatl, gunalchéesh, cháatl." I tell the halibut, "You will feed many children and Elders."

Halibut spring rolls, halibut patty hors d'œuvres, more halibut tacos, halibut fajitas, halibut casserole, dried halibut, halibut pizza, smoked halibut, still more halibut tacos, and halibut crepes.

HALIBUT CREPES

MAKES 4 SERVINGS

*In this fishcamp favorite, delicate homemade crepes are
filled with savory halibut, local greens, and cheese. I like to
make the halibut filling first, then make the crepes. After
the crepes are done, I warm up the halibut filling to fill the
crepes. Some cooks make their crepes ahead of time, even
the day before, and then prepare the filling the day they are
going to serve the meal. Sliced fresh mushrooms and/or
additional seafood like shrimp or crab can be added to the
filling. When I want a little extra richness, I add ½ cup of
cubed cream cheese to the sauce too.*

FOR THE HALIBUT FILLING:

1 large halibut fillet,
about 16 ounces, cooked

¼ cup chopped green or yellow
onions

¼ cup chopped kale or spinach

2 to 3 tablespoons butter

½ cup chicken broth

4 tablespoons all-purpose flour,
plus more if needed

1 cup coconut–almond milk blend
(or substitute heavy cream),
plus more if needed

4 tablespoons plain yogurt, or more
if desired

¼ cup chopped goose tongue
(beach plant)

1 tablespoon chopped spruce tips

¼ cup shredded white cheese of
your choice: Swiss, mozzarella,
Pepper Jack, or blended white
cheeses

FOR THE CREPES:

1 cup all-purpose flour

3 eggs

2 cups coconut or almond milk

4 tablespoons melted butter

Canola oil or melted butter
for cooking

Shredded white cheese for topping
(optional)

Chopped green onions or spinach
(optional)

To make the Halibut Filling, flake or cut the cooked halibut into
small pieces and set aside.

In a frying pan over medium-high heat, sauté the onions and
kale with butter until the onions are no longer translucent and
the kale is wilted, 5 to 7 minutes. Pour ¼ cup of the chicken broth
into a small jar or cup. Add up to 4 tablespoons of flour to the jar
and whisk with a fork to thicken into a paste. Set the paste aside.

Add the remaining ¼ cup of broth, the coconut–almond milk, and yogurt to the pan with the sautéed onions and kale. Mix the flour paste into the pan with a fork.

Reduce the heat to low and stir until the sauce thickens, about 1 to 2 minutes. You can adjust the consistency of the sauce according to your taste—add more milk to make the sauce thinner or add a bit of flour to thicken if necessary. You can also add up to ½ cup plain yogurt if you like more sauce.

Once the sauce thickens, stir in the chopped goose tongue and spruce tips. Gently add the halibut pieces to the sauce. Then stir in the cheese. Set aside.

To make the Crepes, I recommend using a blender to make the crepe batter, but you can also use a bowl and hand mixer.

In a blender or bowl, combine the flour, eggs, milk, and melted butter, and blend or mix until the batter is smooth. Let the batter rest for 2 minutes before cooking. The batter should be thin, so adjust with more milk if necessary.

Set a small or medium frying pan over medium heat and lightly oil or butter. When the pan is hot, pour about half a standard-sized ladleful of batter in the pan and spread it with the bottom of the ladle until the pan is covered with a thin layer of crepe batter. Cook until the bottom of the crepe is lightly browned, about 2 minutes. Loosen the crepe and with a spatula and carefully flip the crepe, cooking the other side for 1 minute. Transfer the cooked crepe to a plate. Continue cooking crepes using the rest of the batter and stacking them on the plate. You can keep the finished crepes warm by placing them in a warm oven with the heat turned off. If you're not filling the crepes right away, drape a warm, slightly damp paper or cloth towel over the plate to keep the crepes warm. The stack of crepes can also be covered on a plate and saved in the fridge for use the next day.

When you're ready to assemble the crepes, make sure the halibut filling is warm and the crepes are cooked. Put a crepe on a plate or clean cutting board. Using a large spoon, fill the lower third of the crepe with the halibut filling and roll the bottom of the crepe upward, like a jellyroll. Sprinkle the extra cheese on top, if using. To melt the cheese atop the crepe, place it on a baking sheet in a warm oven or place the crepe in a warm frying pan off the heat with the lid on for about 1 minute. Repeat with the remaining crepes.

Transfer the crepes to a plate and spoon any remaining filling over the top. Sprinkle chopped green onions or spinach for a garnish and serve right away.

BACKYARD GLACIERS

A new glacier forms when snow remains in the same place all year and enough snow accumulates to transform into ice.

It's August and Vivian and I are riding on the back deck of a jet boat with the breeze in our hair. We're traveling up the Stikine River to Shakes Glacier with Alaska Waters, a local Alaska Native tour company. Vivian is filling in as a cultural guide and I am along for the ride. Guiding visitors has been a tradition in my daughter's family—a relative on her father's side, Sitka Charlie, led John Muir into Glacier Bay.

It grows colder as the boat navigates through Shakes Slough. We slow and motor into Shakes Lake, weaving around icebergs. Visitors gather on the back deck with us, and I hear sighs of amazement as smartphones and cameras are being unzipped from pockets and backpacks.

We pass so close to an iceberg I can smell it. The sensation triggers a memory and I say, "I was born of ice."

A puzzled look crosses my daughter's face.

"My parents moved from Alaska to Hawaii for a few months when they were a young couple," I explain. "My mom, your grandma, was five months pregnant when she started to miscarry. She'd had a miscarriage before. Someone in their apartment complex, an Elder, mentioned an old remedy of packing the abdomen in ice. So they did and it worked. I'm here."

I can't take my eyes away from the blue ice floating on the silty green lake. "I think I imprinted on ice and it imprinted on me," I say.

Every year, snowfall covers the ice and compresses
the layers of snow from previous years.

Shakes Glacier is retreating. Experts say within the next fifteen years, Shakes Glacier will recede far enough to separate from its sources and divide into two glaciers. Eventually it will retract from the lake altogether, making it difficult to access. In addition, the Mendenhall Glacier has retreated two and a half miles since the mid-1700s—one-third of a mile in only the last decade. And then there's the Taku Glacier, southeast of Juneau, one of the thickest alpine glaciers in the world. Once the last advancing glacier, the Taku is also retreating.

Glaciers are a part of my life. My Sámi ancestors' migration story is woven into the receding of glaciers. According to Sámi Oral Tradition, a giant being named Biegolmai, the Wind Man, used two giant shovels to create a glacial landscape. With his first big shovel, he whipped the wind. With the second big shovel, he dropped snowfall after snowfall to create a land that no humans could live on. One day his big wind shovel broke, and the wind died down and it became clear enough for the Sámi to migrate into Sápmi.

Compressing layers on a building glacier makes the snow recrystallize
into a form resembling sugar.

From a safe distance, my daughter and I are silent as we gaze at Shakes Glacier with its rock canyon walls on either side. Carol Williams, a Tradition Bearer from Hoonah, once instructed me that glaciers listen, so we must talk respectfully about glaciers. My children are Tlingit with ancestral roots beginning with glacial activity. Their Clan, T'aḵdeintaan, is from Sít'Eeti Ǥeey, or Glacier Bay.

The grains of ice grow bigger, air pockets between the grains shrink, and the snow slowly compresses, which causes the layers to thicken.

This glacier already knows us, I consider. Drumlins, bands of snow, like tree rings, provide a record of the last ice age within the glacier and the memory of our ecological story. Between the years 1698 and 1948, the annual terminus recession rate of Shakes Glacier was eighty-five feet. From 1948 to 2016, Shakes Glacier retreated at a much faster rate: an average of 350 feet per year!

After about one year, the layers turn into firn, which is well-bonded snow, a state between snow and ice.

The boat motors away from the glacier to a boulder-scoured area near a stream. The captain nudges the boat against the bank and we disembark. We walk around a bit and then it's time for Vivian to give her talk. The visitors gather around as she starts to speak. She explains to her audience that in her culture, before entering a new landscape, one must have an attitude of respect. She speaks in Lingít first, then says in English, "Please forgive me for anything I say or do that might offend people or the animals."

A few small birds fly up from the willows near a stream beyond us, interrupting her talk. Noting the birds were disrupted by a few wandering visitors, she reminds the visitors to be respectful. She points to the birds. "These little kittiwakes are my family. They saved my ancestors from a famine a long time ago."

The age of the oldest glacier ice ever recovered from an Alaskan glacier—from a basin between Mt. Bona and Mt. Churchill in the Saint Elias Mountains in eastern Alaska—is thirty thousand years old.

Vivian introduces herself in the Lingít language. After a couple minutes of introduction, she says in English, "That's Tlingit for hello." She smiles and the visitors laugh.

My daughter's voice rises above the sounds of the wind and the rushing creek. "This river is one of the most beautiful places in the world. We've lived here for more than ten thousand years."

Iceberg floats in Shakes Lake near Shakes Glacier on the Stikine River in the Stikine-LeConte Wilderness. Shakes Glacier is twenty-five miles from Wrangell, Alaska.

She tells them the Tongass rainforest is one of the largest producers of oxygen in the world. "Of course, this air isn't important to just my family—it's important to the entire world. All our ecosystems, we're all attached. It's one planet."

When snow falls on a glacier and is compressed,
air bubbles are squeezed out and the ice crystals enlarge.
This makes the ice appear blue.

Vivian continues, explaining the Tongass National Forest is one of the most diverse ecosystems left. She shows them alders, willows, and cottonwoods and describes how they're medicine trees. She talks about the importance of the Stikine River to the Tahltan, Tlingit, Haida, and Tsimshian. And lastly, she thanks them for taking the time to visit this beautiful place. "Gunalchéesh," she says.

Glaciers are the largest source of fresh water on the planet,
storing 75 percent of the earth's fresh water.

After her talk and a bit of exploring the river's shore, we get back onto the boat and settle in for the trip back. As we head out of Shakes Lake and past the icebergs, I take a last look at Shakes Glacier. I address it according to protocol: "Gunalchéesh, Léelk'w." Thank you, Grandmother, for providing us safe passage.

Looking back over our boat's wake, I marvel at this glacier. She's an old grandmother. Grandmother, you're as ancient as bits of pine needles and alder pollen—articles kept in your medicine bag. You hold a pine needle from a fall storm that thundered through five hundred years ago, a sliver of cedar from the raft that floated local Clans down beneath the ice, and pollen spores from ten thousand years ago. I wonder if you're recording our visit this day.

TOTE ICE

There's nothing like the chill at the face of a glacier,
and there's nothing like chilling out with friends
and eating a picnic on a sandbar or at a cabin.

1 skiff

1 iceberg

1 dip net

1 cooler

Steer your skiff toward a small floating chunk of iceberg. Be careful—icebergs are large underneath and can damage your propeller. Have someone else on board scoop up some ice with a dip net or another contraption, or by hand. Put the chunks of the glacier ice in your cooler. Ice that's been here for thousands of years will keep your snacks or beverages chilled for a few days.

TEA FOR COMMUNITY

Grandson Jackson stands holding a pink blossom that if ingested could cause a drop in blood pressure, vomiting, and death. In his other hand is a sprig of the white-blossomed s'ikshaldéen (Labrador tea or Hudson Bay tea) we're harvesting for our community.

My dad, Jackson, and I have stopped at the Upper Salamander Creek camping area. We walk down the trail to the muskeg. This bog is accessible for kids and Elders. Great-grandpa Mickey stops to rest and tell a story of how he fell in the muskeg once and nearly died because he couldn't get out. My favorite name for Labrador tea is Storytelling Tea. Grandson Jackson and I listen. Afterward, we step into the muskeg wearing boots and rain gear, as gathering tea after the rain is wet work.

Across the muskeg, white and pink flowers bloom, perfuming the July morning. "Try not to step on the plants," I tell Jackson, though I know it's impossible. We practice saying the Lingít word: s'ikshaldéen (sick-shuth-DEAN). S'ikshaldéen is known by other names such as tundra tea, Indian tea, marsh tea, swamp tea, St. James's tea, Haida tea, and more.

We step gingerly, our boots sinking. I pick a pink-blossomed plant and a white-blossomed plant, both growing near each another.

Two similar-looking pink plants that grow in the area, bog

rosemary (*Andromeda polifolia*) and bog laurel (*Kalmia microphylla* var. *occidentalis*), are both toxic. We examine a pink flower. "Pink, poisonous," I say. "Easy to remember. And there's white underneath and the leaves are kind of shiny."

I hold the white-blossomed one and turn it over. It has narrow, one-inch leaves. I pick a leaf. The top is smooth, the edges a bit turned under. Rusty-orange hairs on the underside act like a sponge, helping the plant retain moisture from the muskeg and rain. We inspect the leaf. "An orange belly is good," I say. "Belly is good for making jelly."

Jackson holds up the pink blossom. "Poisonous pink," he says. He holds up the white-blossomed sprig. "White blossoms and an orange belly mean it's good." Got it!

We walk to a large patch with the plants growing in different heights. S'ikshaldéen is in the same family as rhododendrons and azaleas. It can grow to several feet high, but in colder climates it grows lower, forming a carpet. It's especially adaptive and fire tolerant. It will resprout from stems in a low-intensity fire. If a fire destroys the top, s'ikshaldéen rapidly regenerates from the roots and rhizomes, which are sometimes two feet down.

Labrador tea is high in vitamin C and can be made into a syrup for coughs and sore throats. It's a commonly used medicine among Arctic peoples and Northwest Coast Tribes. The tea is used to treat the flu, stomach problems, muscle spasms, arthritis, hangovers, and head lice. It can be used as a bath for eczema, and medicinal properties in the leaves and stems are being studied for anti-tumor capabilities. But Auntie Viv warns that Labrador tea is unsafe in large or concentrated amounts because it can cause stomach inflammation, vomiting, gastroenteritis, diarrhea, and more. And it's unsafe to use while pregnant or breastfeeding.

I touch a spindly plant blooming with white flowers and pull it toward us. Jackson bends near. I pluck a few leaves from the top. "See how this one is spindly and tall, and those are full of leaves? This one should be pruned," I explain.

Some harvesters avoid picking the plant during its bloom, which is typically May through July. Others, including Auntie Viv, make tea from the white blossoms. "People like us and the animals," I say to Jackson, "the caribou, moose, and migrating birds browse on the tea.

Even the wind helps prune."

My rule is to take only a few new shoots from each area, and don't take all the leaves when harvesting older leaves. We harvest a small bagful, and then the three of us hop back into the truck and ride along the dirt road, looking for another muskeg. A mile or so down the road, a sasquatch catches our attention. It peers out menacingly from the tree line, its familiar stance made famous by a well-known bigfoot photo.

"I can't believe it!" Jackson exclaims.

"Maybe the Forest Service's mascot is now a bigfoot," I say, laughing.

We get out of the truck and Jackson and I step across the ditch. We don't approach the large wooden bigfoot, but decide this is an interesting place to harvest. My dad stays harvesting tea near the muskeg edge. As we pick, I talk about how harvesting protocols differ with each Tribe and sometimes with each family. Jackson's Chippewa relatives harvest differently from his Tlingit relatives. I mention that even our Sámi relatives use the tea.

After a few muskegs, we've picked a couple gallons. The leaves will rot if left in a plastic bag; they need to be dried or frozen. I dry Labrador tea in paper bags in a warm place, on a baking sheet in the sun, or in a food dehydrator. If it's humid, I dry it on a low temperature in the oven. Dried tea lasts most of the year or even longer. Crumble it up and put it in jars for seasoning. I sometimes freeze spring growth and the dried tea in small amounts. Most importantly, we share it with community: our Elders, the auntie who makes our medicines, the Clan sister who moved to New Jersey, and anyone who can't get out to harvest themselves.

Making tea is an art. There are several methods of doing it, but boiling Labrador tea leaves releases toxic alkaloids, so it's recommended to pour boiling water over the leaves and steep them for about five to ten minutes and no longer. Use it as an herbal tea for what ails us and as a spice to flavor meat. My family tucks sprigs behind our ears and puts it in jars of water and scatters leaves across the table at our campsites to keep bugs away. I use it in pesto, chop it into muffins and breads, and add a sprig to my water for flavor.

Labrador tea is an evergreen and doesn't shed leaves. This

Labrador tea blossoms surround a basket of Labrador tea in the muskeg.

adaptation allows the plant to keep warm in northern climates and retain moisture. Harvesting it depends on your preferences. We harvest year round, depending on our needs. Spring growth tastes slightly different from earthy-tasting fall growth, and the medicinal properties are different too. Spring growth also doesn't have the orange underside, so when identifying it make sure to look at the older leaves and note the blossoms' color, if any. We harvest new growth by pinching *above* where the new growth begins because the blossoms' health depends on the previous year's growth—dormant buds are beneath the joint.

In springtime, when I walk in the muskeg, I want to lie down and rest in the intoxicating scent. In the fall, the tea scent is deep and woodsy and familiar. It's the smell of dried tea leaves many Alaskans grew up with.

Grandson Jackson, my dad, and I walk among the leaves, picking and telling stories. This is our tea ceremony: we pick new growth in the spring and early summer, and older growth in the fall. Our next excursion for tea will be soon. We will head out in Dís Yádi (Child Moon), September, when many harvesters traditionally pick

Labrador tea. It's also the month "when food begins to be scarce and we do with less."

If you receive a small bag of handpicked dried tea, think about footprints sunk into bog, about small hands and large hands working together, about fingers pinching off leaves, about kneeling and touching the earth, about taking care and giving. Labrador tea is a tea for community. If you take a friend, a grandchild, or an Elder with you when you gather the leaves, a story of community will weave itself among the moss and bull pine and eventually steep in the bottom of a cup—it's teatime.

LABRADOR TEA

MAKES 4 CUPS

My favorite name for Labrador tea is Storytelling Tea.
It's great to drink all year round and is so easy to make.
You've worked hard harvesting this tea from the muskeg.
Make it for a friend, sit down together, and let
the stories flow over the earthy-tasting beverage.

4 cups water
¼ cup Labrador tea leaves
   (20 to 30 leaves)

Bring the water to a boil in a kettle or pot. Meanwhile, place the Labrador tea leaves in a heatproof bowl. Pour the boiling water over the leaves and steep for 5 to 10 minutes. Using a slotted spoon, remove the leaves from the tea.

To serve, fill one-third of a teacup with the steeped tea and the remaining two-thirds with more hot water. Serve hot.

ENCOUNTERS WITH THE GIANT PACIFIC OCTOPUS

Grandfather is fishing for king salmon on the Mercedes, *his forty-foot wooden troller.* The boat rocks and he turns toward the jerking lines. He reels in the gurdies and as the lines come up, he sees it: a giant Pacific octopus. It's monstrous, its skin humanlike in texture and tinged with pink and purple. He unhooks it and it flops onto the deck hatch and reaches its arms outward. Grandfather backs up against the pilothouse. A tentacle moves toward him as if it can sense him there. He readies his knife. The tentacle arm reaches Grandfather's feet and moves up his pant leg, feeling along. It reaches for his bicep and feels his shoulder. Grandfather resists the urge to slice it as the arm moves toward his face. He holds his breath. The octopus taps Grandfather's cheek, then moves downward again, tracing his hip, down his leg, and finally moving away across the deck. Grandfather exhales—he can breathe again.

Grandfather stays pressed against the pilothouse, watching. The octopus reaches to spread one arm to the starboard side and another to the port side: a twelve-foot span. The creature touches the ocean water over both sides of the boat, feeling its lifeline, then pulls its eight arms together, stiffens them, and pushes off, heaving its body overboard. With hardly a splash, the octopus descends beneath the surface of the green water.

Grandfather told this story to his wide-eyed son, my father, and my father told it to me. The creature my grandfather hooked on his trolling gear was a giant Pacific octopus, *Enteroctopus dofleini*, the largest octopus in the world. The giant Pacific octopus can grow up to thirty feet long. They weigh on average between one hundred to two hundred pounds. Not surprisingly, the Tlingit call the large octopus náakw (knockw), or "devilfish." Giant octopuses occupy my worldview; they're a part of my heritage. In the Finnish national epic work the *Kalevala*, there's a creature referred to as Iku-Turso, a giant octopus or a combination of walrus and octopus. And then there's the Kraken, a Scandinavian mythological sea monster which is sometimes depicted as an octopus or giant squid.

My children's people, the Tlingit, and my ancestors, the Sámi and Suomalaiset, have relied on the ocean's bounty for thousands of years, so it's no wonder many of our stories dwell on the sea. We think of the octopus as strictly being an ocean dweller, but what if they do come ashore occasionally? My daughter Vivian says her paternal grandfather, Elmer Mork, has been telling her all her life that octopuses walk on land. He said no one believed him. He told her a story about a time when he and his brother Ray were young and out exploring the beach near the cannery in Hoonah. There they saw an octopus walk up the beach to the tree line and eat blueberries. They caught the octopus and killed it so they could eat it. When they told the story to their mother, Eliza Mork got mad at them. She said, "It was a special octopus. When you see animals doing human things, you leave them alone." When I think of this admonition, I'm certain there's more to this creature than we understand.

My first encounter with an octopus occurred when I was around four years old. As children, my sister and I would go shrimping with my maternal grandfather and on one occasion the trawl pulled up a small octopus among the thousands of wiggling shrimp. My grandfather put the octopus in a five-gallon bucket. We touched it and giggled, but the creature needed to return to the sea, so we let it go. I still recall how my fingertips touched the octopus's tentacles and how I sensed it was also touching me.

An octopus has an extremely sensitive sense of touch, the rims of its suckers being the most sensitive. A new study about how octopuses process information has revealed they have intelligence similar to ravens and primates. Octopuses have neurons and suckers in their arms in addition to their brain. They "feel" and "taste" the world in order to know it, which is what the octopus was doing on the deck of Grandpa's boat—learning about and tasting the fisherman who'd just accidentally plopped it on the back deck of his troller. It's likely that my grandfather's intimate encounter with a giant octopus on his boat was just as terrifyingly wonderful for the octopus.

I dream I'm walking the dock in Sitka's harbor. I see my daughter Vivian on the stern of her liveaboard boat, leaning over the ocean speaking to a giant Pacific octopus. She has her iPhone out and is narrating the encounter on a live feed. The octopus is one of Vivian's Clan crests so it doesn't really surprise me, but I'm still apprehensive, even a little scared. I don't want her to fall in and I'm not sure of the octopus's intentions. It is huge and has an orange-pinkish color. It moves its giant tentacles about as it communicates with her. The octopus is holding something bright green in its tentacles. I look harder and realize it's a book—my poetry collection *The Hide of My Tongue*, about Lingít language loss and revitalization. Evidently, my daughter is teaching the octopus Lingít words and has gifted the octopus my poetry. The book is getting wet as the octopus holds it. Then, as if to say thank you, the octopus reaches up and gently pats my daughter's face. I wake up and lie there as if floating on the sea.

Later, I have my morning coffee and I check my Facebook feed to discover a memory from six years prior—it's the publication anniversary of my poetry collection, the same one the giant octopus was holding in my dream. The strange thing is, I wasn't thinking about the book last night—I didn't even remember its publication date. I hadn't talked about it recently either, and I hadn't seen anything on social media about it. Evidently, the octopus in my dream knew what day it was.

Octopus dreams and encounters are always open for speculation. My grandfather's encounter with a giant octopus is certainly fascinating. Maybe, after it met my grandfather that day on the boat, the octopus swam home and told others of its adventure. Maybe it described how it reached its long arm across the boat and patted up the curve of a bipedal creature's legs, touched its bony hip, tapped its face where it rolled its sucker cups over a stubbled cheek and thumped a dimpled chin. As the giant Pacific octopus patted Grandfather's chest, its neurons fired as it felt his beating heart. The octopus likely knew this strange creature was alive and afraid— perhaps as afraid and anxious as the octopus was. And maybe at that moment, the curious octopus decided to leap back into the sea.

SMOKED OCTOPUS SALAD

MAKES 4 SERVINGS

Yes, we eat octopus. If we aren't out specifically fishing for them and catch one, sometimes we let the octopus go. But if the octopus is injured by the hook, it's disrespectful not to eat it. Octopus can be a gift because we might not have had octopus in a while, or because we plan to take food to a memorial or other ceremony. Like other seafood, octopus blends well with citrusy flavors. The citrus, spruce tips, and vinegar in the dressing give the octopus salad a fresh zing.

FOR THE ORANGE–SPRUCE TIP DRESSING:

2 tablespoons finely chopped spruce tips

⅓ cup freshly squeezed orange juice

2 tablespoons white wine vinegar

1 tablespoon avocado oil

1 tablespoon raw honey

1 teaspoon Spruce Tip Juice (page 20) (optional)

Salt and freshly ground black pepper to taste

FOR THE OCTOPUS SALAD:

2 tablespoons lemon juice

1 teaspoon paprika

1 cup freshly cooked or smoked octopus (or substitute canned octopus)

1 bunch fresh spinach

1 bunch arugula

1 small can olives (any kind), sliced

1 cup whole cherry tomatoes

1 avocado, sliced

½ cup diced English cucumber

½ cup chopped seaweed

½ cup hand-torn goose tongue or green onions

To make the Orange–Spruce Tip Dressing, in a blender or bowl, combine the spruce tips, orange juice, vinegar, avocado oil, honey, and Spruce Tip Juice, if using. Blend until smooth, or immerse an immersion blender in the mixture and mix until smooth. Season with salt and black pepper to taste. Set aside.

To make the Octopus Salad, drizzle lemon juice and sprinkle the paprika onto the octopus, then set aside. In a bowl, combine the spinach, arugula, olives, cherry tomatoes, avocado, cucumber, seaweed, and goose tongue and toss well. Divide the salad mixture among serving plates and scatter the seasoned octopus over the top. Drizzle with the Orange–Spruce Tip Dressing and serve right away.

RED HUCKLEBERRY:
FOOD FOR SONGBIRDS

Red huckleberry sauce on salmon, shrimp, and crab, red huckleberry-stuffed halibut rolls, in spring rolls, in salads, dipping sauce for sushi.

My dad slows "Huckleberry"—his bright-red side-by-side four-wheeler—to a stop alongside the dirt road. I climb out of the passenger seat and my dog Oscar jumps out behind me. I grab my backpack, stuff a bucket into it, and hang another bucket around my neck. Before me is a hillside of stumps, fallen logs, and bushes. Bejeweled huckleberry bushes dot the hillside. It's fall—time to pick red huckleberries for making jams and jellies and to store for winter.

I've trained my eyes to spot the difference between a blueberry and a red huckleberry bush; in summer, the red huckleberries' green leaves are slightly smaller than those of the blueberry and there are more leaves on its bushes. It's easier to tell them apart in the late summer and early fall when the red huckleberry leaves turn redder. In any season, to find red huckleberries, look near stump patches, as they tend to grow in places where trees have fallen. They are also found at the edges of muskegs, often tucked beneath a hemlock or spruce. They grow down the coast from Southeast Alaska to as far away as Central California.

Red huckleberry jam or jelly.

I am wearing a ballcap, rain pants, and a raincoat because yesterday it poured, and the bushes are soaked. My dad heads to pick from the lower bushes beside the small parking area. I cross the road, step across the ditch, and climb onto the hill, steadying myself by grabbing onto a small tree branch. Berry picking is hard work, but worth it. I stop at a bush about five feet high, thick with plump, red berries.

The Lingít word for red huckleberry, tleikatánk, which sounds like tl-ache-uh-TUNK. In the online Tlingit dictionary published by Sealaska, you'll find these sentences: "Tleikatánk kanat'á een yak'éi" (Red huckleberries are good with blueberries) and "Tleikatánk áwé kanat'áx̱ x̱oo yéi nateech" (Red huckleberries are always among blueberries). This is Traditional Knowledge—when scouting for blueberries you'll often discover a patch of red huckleberries.

Red huckleberry muffins, bread, cobbler, buckle, and pie.

I find my footing and pull a loaded branch toward me. Oscar sniffs the grass. I pick a few berries and plop them into a bucket, making a hollow sound. Somewhere behind me, a blue jay squawks. I sing to Oscar, to the birds and the berries, letting the creatures know I'm around. There's something for me to sing about here in the bushes, surrounded by dripping berries and leaves, the repetitive motion of finding berries with my fingertips and plunking them into my buckets. I'd rather be in this moment than anywhere else. As my grandsons often say, "This is the best day of my life."

A raven's waterdrop call—it sounds like water dripping from a faucet—carries across the road from the towering cedar and hemlocks. Ravens probably like the bright red huckleberries too. They are an important food for local songbirds. I've seen birds fly out from bushes with these berries in their beaks. Deer love to graze on the berries, leaves, and stems. Red huckleberries are a significant part of the diet of bears, grouse, and squirrels too.

Red huckleberry iced tea, smoothies, lemonade, tea, and milkshakes.

Yesterday's rain drips like jewels from the berries. I pop a couple of leaves in my mouth and chew them. Indigenous Peoples of the Pacific Northwest use red huckleberry leaves for medicine. You can boil the bark and make a tea to treat colds. The leaves and stems can be chopped and used to treat gout. The leaves are also used as a medicinal tea for lowering or modifying blood sugar levels.

A handful of fresh red huckleberries in oatmeal, cereal, water, or yogurt.

After picking for a couple of hours, Dad and I drive Huckleberry back to the truck, load her onto the trailer, and head back to our fishcamp. Next week we'll be making our jams and jellies.

You can dry red huckleberries by either laying them on a cloth and setting them in the sun for a couple of days, using a food dehydrator, or drying them in the oven on a very low temperature with the oven door left open a crack. Dried red huckleberries can be stored like you'd store raisins and will last up to two years in the freezer. And of course, you'll want to eat them freshly dried, or make something out of them to share. They're rich in vitamin C and fiber, great nutrients during winter.

Red huckleberry in oatmeal bars, oatmeal cookies,
and huckleberry upside-down cake.

For the best red huckleberries, stay in tune with the current season and keep watch on your favorite patch. Though they ripen from July through September, picking them later means they'll be plumper and less tart—I've picked them as late as the first week of October. Some people freeze the berries individually on trays before they package them up.

Red huckleberry sorbet, ice cream, tarts,
croissants, fry bread, and donuts.

Wrangell has quite a lot of red huckleberries—the bushes love our wet coastal climate—but the patches are closely guarded secrets. Many harvesters reserve their knowledge for family and friends. Take time to scout out the patches respectfully; if you find an easy patch, make sure it's not a local Elder's favorite patch. Invite a friend, relative or Elder, anyone with limited abilities. Don't forget to bring kids and dogs and a lunch. Wrangell is fortunate to have picnicking areas with accessible picnic tables, parking spots, and berry patches. Your companions can help with picking, sorting leaves, keeping watch, telling stories, and even singing to make your presence known.

Finally, remember when you're out picking red huckleberries not to deplete the whole spot. After all, red huckleberries are an essential food for brown bears and songbirds. And remember, the best day of your life will be one spent in berry bushes dripping with rain, with a dog at your feet and the tart-sweet taste of a juicy red huckleberry in your mouth, thinking about making a red huckleberry pie.

Red huckleberry pancakes, syrup, scones, and cream cheese pie.

Mickey Prescott's original huckleberry dream pie made from freshly picked red huckleberries.

MICKEY'S HUCKLEBERRY DREAM PIE

MAKES 1 PIE

This pie is my dad's favorite—he invented it himself. It features a quickly cooked foraged-berry compote contrasted with a cheesecake-like filling, nestled in a graham cracker crust. Since red huckleberries ripen in late summer, it's the perfect dessert for end-of-summer picnics or fall family celebrations. My older sister Joy also taught my dad how to make a blueberry version. There's nothing quite like eating a pie made from berries you and your loved ones just freshly picked.

4 cups red huckleberries (or substitute blueberries)

1 cup sugar

3 tablespoons cornstarch

2 (8-ounce) packages cream cheese, softened

1 teaspoon vanilla extract

1 prepared graham cracker crust

Whipped cream for serving (optional)

In a saucepan over medium heat, combine the red huckleberries, ½ cup of the sugar, and the cornstarch. Bring the mixture to a boil while stirring constantly until the mixture thickens, about 3 minutes. Remove from the heat and set aside to cool.

In a large bowl, combine the cream cheese, remaining ½ cup sugar, and the vanilla. Mix with an electric mixer until fluffy, about 2 minutes. Carefully spread the mixture across the bottom and up the sides of the graham cracker crust to form a bowl of cream cheese. Pour the cooled berry mixture into the center of the cream cheese layer and carefully even it out to the edges with a rubber spatula or spoon. Chill the pie into the refrigerator until set, about 2 hours.

Cut the pie into wedges and serve as is or with whipped cream.

WRANGELL WINTER GAMES

We look toward Grandson Jonah, ready to roll the bones. He holds six dice in his small hands, and as he shakes them his whole body vibrates. He's learning to play ten thousand, a favorite family winter game. Ten thousand is also called zilch or farkle. We wait for Jonah to let go of the dice. He shakes and shakes until his mother, Nikka, is laughing so hard she can't speak to remind him to actually throw the dice. Finally, he opens his hands, and the dice topple as if in slow motion onto the table.

Dice have held the power to determine inheritances, predict the future, and even choose who ruled a kingdom. What you rolled was once considered to be controlled by gods. Today Lady Luck favors Grandson Jonah. "You have a thousand! You're on the board!" we cheer. We show him which numbers to look for: ones and fives and three of a kind. He's starting the game off well, but in a few rounds his attention span will likely wane, and he'll go join his cousins playing and dancing on the Wii in the adjoining room.

The first mention of card playing was in the year 868 CE, when Princess Tong Chen of China played a leaf game with her family.

Every Friday night, four generations of our family gather to play cards, dice, and board games at my sister's house. It started after my sister and I moved back home to Wrangell following our retirements and our grown children moved back "home" to raise their families here. Originally it came about because we needed something to do on winter nights, but game night soon evolved to something we do year round, including outside in midsummer on my sister's patio. Game night is not just for games but for sharing stories and food. We've planned menus of seafood, pizza, soup and bread, and even a bacon theme, as well as foods from Mexico, India, and the Philippines. And we always have iced tea or lemonade made from local berries.

Some sports or games like horse racing is illegal in Alaska,
but the state allows dog mushing and other games
associated with nature and local cultures.

In Alaska there are local bingo halls everywhere. There are classics, or guessing games: the Canned Salmon Classic, a couple of goose classics, a king salmon classic, a cabbage classic, a rain classic, a snow machine classic, and the Deep Freeze Classic. There are competitions like fishing derbies and bull moose derbies, and lotteries like a mushing sweepstakes. Social in-home gambling is allowed, so we're good. All we're doing now is spitting in the ocean.

Spit in the ocean was our Grandpa Pressy's favorite poker game, and my sister has memories of playing it with him. It's a card game with huge pots of money—or candy, in our case—at stake. Each player is dealt a hand of cards facedown and combines them with faceup cards on the table to make a poker hand. And yes, someone usually pretends to spit in the ocean.

Before television came to town in the 1960s, Wrangellites played cards and board games at different neighbors' houses. People met regularly for cribbage, pinochle, and rummy known by different names: frustration, fascination, Shanghai, contract, progressive, and May I? Various types of games rolled through our house like fads: blackout, nertz, and mancala. Aggravation, a marble board game, was one of our favorites. Sometime in the late 1970s, Liverpool rummy swept everyone up in its vortex. A makeshift shack served as the harbor office for an out-the-road harbor doubled as the venue for late-night, card-filled extravaganzas. What began as a way to

Game night. Left to right: Nikka Mork (author's daughter), Ed Bruns (author's brother-in-law), Joy Prescott (author's sister), Mickey Prescott (author's father), Breanne Pearson (author's daughter), and Nick Pearson (author's son-in-law).

pass the time during the dark winter grew to folks of all ages sitting shoulder to shoulder and shooting the breeze. As fishermen laid down two sets and a run, they'd tell you where the good spots to drag your shrimp trawl were.

Dominoes possibly descended from dice games in China and spread to the West during the eighteenth century.

Tonight my sister has brought Chicken Foot, a dominoes game, back from her trip to Seattle. I figure it must be fancy having come from the city, but when my sister spreads out the tiles facedown and explains the rules, I think it's just a kids game. Later I learn that Chicken Foot likely originated from Texas or even Mexico and is similar to a game I know as Maltese cross. We each pick our tiles from a pile in the center of the table and set them on their edges in front of us so the other players can't see them. The object of the game is to play all the dominoes in your hand and get a low score.

My sister shows us how to make a chicken foot with a double-value domino. "You have to say 'chicken foot' when you make one, and then everyone plays off of your foot," she says. "Oh, and you have to cluck like a chicken," she adds, "when you run out of tiles."

The game progresses and when almost all the tiles are almost used up, my dad bends his arm in a wing-shape. "Cluck cluck!" he says. He's out of tiles. We play more rounds and sip iced tea and invent new versions of the game we might play the next time—dinosaur foot, unicorn foot, salmon foot. We laugh trying to figure out what salmon might say in place of cluck cluck.

The longest Monopoly game was played for seventy straight days.

Sometimes we end our game nights with my dad's favorite game: sequence. He's good at it and he wins a lot. Sequence is a game of strategy, wits, and luck, a mix of bingo and cards using poker chips. It has it all.

"Sequence!" my dad exclaims. This is the second time he's won. Time to go home. It's 8 p.m., which is usually when we call it quits after playing games for several hours.

"Aww," says one of the disappointed grandkids.

Our winter games do not consist of the luge or curling, and we don't get medals. Food is our opening ceremony and laughter is our prize. A few hours of laughter and games and we remember why family is important.

Sometimes on game nights I lean over and pretend to spit in the ocean. My sister clucks like a chicken. My dad tells a fishing story. Jonah shakes his whole body, and the dice go rolling round the floor. Nikka laughs. My niece Rhiannon and my grandsons Timothy and Jackson wiggle their bodies, dancing on the Wii to a disco beat.

We roll away the game board, put the game chips into their bags. In a few days' time, we'll be texting one another, planning the next game night: "Who's bringing the shrimp sandwiches?"

SHRIMP SANDWICHES

MAKES 8 OPEN-FACED SANDWICHES

I come from a family of commercial shrimpers. Some of my first memories are being on the back deck of my grandfather's shrimp boat. We shrimpers like the wild flavor of Alaskan shrimp to shine through in our recipes. Feel free to bring your own favorite ingredients to the mix; I like adding chopped jalapeño, goose tongue, or spruce tips to my sandwich filling.

2 cups cooked shrimp

2 green onions, chopped

1 celery stalk, chopped

4 ounces cream cheese, softened but not melted, plus more if needed

¼ cup mayonnaise, plus more if needed

¼ teaspoon freshly ground black pepper

Dash of garlic powder

Dash of Lawry's or Johnny's Seasoning Salt

Pinch of paprika

8 slices white sandwich bread; baguettes or French bread will also work

Sliced green olives, for topping

In a food processor, combine the shrimp, green onions, celery, cream cheese, mayonnaise, black pepper, garlic powder, your choice of seasoning salt, and paprika. (If you are including other additions, add them now.) Process everything to your preferred spread consistency, whether that's chunky or smooth. Transfer the mixture a bowl. You can adjust the spreadability by adding more cream cheese or mayonnaise.

Divide the mixture among the 8 bread slices and cut the slices into quarters, or use a cookie cutter to make fun shapes. Top with sliced green olives and garnish with a sprinkle of paprika. (Alternatively, you can spread the mixture on 4 bread slices and top with the rest of the bread slices.) Serve immediately.

WINTER STORIES

"We had some pretty tough winters in the old days," my dad says. "I once walked a couple hundred yards across the harbor from the Fish & Game float to Reliance float. The harbor was frozen to the breakwater."

"Let's go look for winter," I tell my dad. I want to photograph the muskeg in all its winter finery. More than 10 percent of Southeast Alaska is covered in muskeg and Wrangell Island has a lot of it. It's especially beautiful in winter, with frost-covered moss and trees and a blanket of sparkling snow. With Huckleberry—my dad's red four-wheeler—in tow on a trailer, we make it out the main logging road to the turnoff on the backside of Nemo Loop. We pull into a small parking area and unload Huckleberry. I get in and Oscar stops barking at the four-wheeler and jumps in beside me, waiting for a ride.

"Winter sure is pretty," I say as we wait for the cab to warm up. Around us, cedar and hemlock sparkle silvery blue in the noonday sun. "Seems like it's going to be a mild winter, maybe. Not like the one where you dug out the frozen sewer?"

My dad laughs. He knows I want to hear the full story, one about "the old days."

He indulges me:

"One year the whole town stayed frozen from October until April. It was fifteen below zero in mid-November when I was working the green chain at the mill. That was the year of the big earthquake. The sewer pipe from our house to the road froze up, and the sewage was backing up into the house. There was a foot of ice on the road. I chopped the ice out and found a manhole. The manhole was twelve feet deep and it was frozen all the way to the top with sewage. I went down to city hall and said, 'I could use some help.' But they said no because they were too busy. The whole town was frozen."

"So, how long did it take you to thaw the sewer line out?" I ask.

"I used an ax, rock salt, and de-icer to get the sewer thawed. I had to dig all that sewage out of the manhole. As it turned out, chunks of water pipe from a blasting project up the road in a new subdivision had floated down into the sewer lines and blocked them. That's why the sewer backed up and froze. It took me a day to dig the manhole out. That's how I spent the weekend: fixing the sewer."

The cab is now warm enough and we take off down the road. We bump along in the snowy ruts until we find a muskeg. My dad turns off the engine and I say, "This looks good." I get out of the four-wheeler, and Oscar and I venture into the muskeg. My dad stands at the edge of the muskeg. With his new hearing aids, he's listening to crackling ice and the way frost sounds under his feet. Oscar and I step gingerly around the frozen ponds, which don't look solid enough to hold us.

Near one pond, I get down on my knees. My reflection is broken in the pond's icy surface. The landscape appears like a miniature world with frozen trees, which are really blades of grass growing from the ice. All around, Labrador tea plants with their frosty hats seem to be dancing at a fairy ball. How can there be so much life in the muskeg with its perpetual state of decay? I expected the muskeg in winter to be frozen, in stasis, with everything just waiting for spring. But now I realize the muskeg is reminding me we're a part of a great, big organic story about living and dying. Winter, a season we often associate with aging and death, is truly beautiful.

The bull pines are covered in frost and I take photo after photo. I love bull pines. These grandparent trees are very old—some live over three hundred years. These old trees listen to us walk in the muskeg. They've listened to our stories, seen our breath cloud up and float across to that lone frost-crusted leaf hanging on the alder branch.

These trees will outlive my dad, who's in his winter of life. The trees will outlive me too. Winter is beautiful but a bit melancholy.

We get back into the four-wheeler and my dad drives us further. After a few minutes, he slows down, stops, opens the cab door, and looks down at the snow. "Moose tracks," he says. I jump out, run around to his side, and look down. Oscar follows me, sniffing the tracks. Sure enough, there are tracks with two large, pointed toes. My dad is a good tracker. I take photos before getting back into the four-wheeler, but after a mile or so the road is impassable and we decide to turn around.

Back at the truck we decide to eat the sandwiches and sliced apples I've brought along before loading up the four-wheeler. I like hanging out with my dad in the wilderness because I'm always gifted a story. Sometimes it's one I've heard dozens of times. Other times it's a story I haven't heard before, like this one:

"My dad, your grandfather, was out fishing in his troller, the *Mercedes*, and Ed Loftus, his fishing partner, was out in his own troller. They were down Back Channel and anchored up on the mainland shore for the night. When they woke up in the morning, they found the whole Back Channel had frozen during the night. They were stuck! They went to the beach and cut down two spruce trees. They tied them on each side of the *Mercedes*. They tied them up at the waterline and brought the tips forward to the front to make an ice plow. The *Mercedes* broke the ice for Ed and his boat, who followed my dad back home. The *Mercedes* was an icebreaker!"

I laugh at the image in my mind, the *Mercedes* breaking ice, another troller close behind in its ice-free wake.

We load Huckleberry onto the trailer and head back to town. Wintertime is for remembering and also for making new stories. Along the way another story thaws and crystallizes in the truck cab. My dad tells me, "The City used to run out of water when it got really cold. They'd take a pump out to Pats Crick and fill tanks and large wooden tierces and deliver water. The town sold water out of plastic garbage cans. The city would come to your house and pump water into your can for you."

As my dad tells the story, I look out the window and consider *this* is my dad's winter story—wandering through forests and muskegs, driving the logging roads, a winter picnic, ancient bull pines covered in frost, moose tracks, and a dangling alder cone glinting with ice crystals.

SALMON PATTIES

MAKES 6 PATTIES

Serve these with rice tossed with chopped spruce tips and sprinkled with fireweed blossoms. Two pint-sized Mason jars of salmon makes about 6 salmon patties, but you can vary the size of the patties for serving or make mini-patties for hors d'oeuvres. Dip your salmon patties in the Spruce Tip Tartar Sauce and/or the Fireweed Dipping Sauce. Serve leftover salmon patties cold between slices of your favorite bread or in a hamburger bun.

2 (16-ounce) jars smoked salmon, 4 cups cooked flaked salmon, or 2 (14- or 16-ounce) cans store-bought salmon

½ cup chopped yellow onion

½ cup fireweed blossoms

¼ cup fresh cilantro, beach lovage, or parsley

6 to 8 crackers of your choice, or ¼ cup cornmeal (plus more for crunchier patties)

6 whole spruce tips

1 to 2 eggs

¼ teaspoon paprika

Handful goose tongue or other beach greens

Dash of garlic powder

Freshly ground black pepper

Lawry's or Johnny's Seasoning Salt to taste

Mayonnaise, if needed

Canola oil for frying

If using a food processor, combine the salmon, onion, fireweed blossoms, cilantro, crackers, spruce tips, and 1 egg. Add the paprika, goose tongue, garlic powder, black pepper, and seasoning salt; if using smoked salmon, use a light hand with the seasoning. Process for 20 seconds, then pulse until the mixture is a consistency that holds together when pressed between your fingers.

If making the patties in a bowl with a fork, chop the onions, fireweed blossoms, cilantro, spruce tips, and goose tongue to a fine consistency and combine in the bowl. Crumble the crackers in by hand, and add the salmon, 1 egg, paprika, garlic powder, black pepper, and seasoning salt; if using smoked salmon, use a light hand with the seasoning. Mix with a fork until the mixture is completely blended and there are no visibly large chunks of flaky fish and cracker crumbs.

Test the consistency of the mixture by pressing a bit of it in your hands. It should stick together and hold a shape. If it falls apart easily, then add another egg or a tablespoon of mayonnaise and mix well. Divide the mixture into 6 equal portions. Roll about ⅓ to ½ cup of mixture into balls and flatten in the palm of your hand. If you want hors d'oeuvres size, then make them smaller. If you want crunchier salmon patties, gently coat the patties in cornmeal.

In a frying pan over medium-high heat, warm ¼ cup of the oil until shimmering. Add the patties and fry until crisp and browned, 2 to 4 minutes. Flip the patties and fry until cooked through and browned on the other side, 2 to 4 more minutes.

Serve warm with Spruce Tip Tartar Sauce or Fireweed Dipping Sauce.

SPRUCE TIP TARTAR SAUCE

½ to 1 cup mayonnaise

2 tablespoons finely chopped dill or sweet pickles or relish

2 tablespoons chopped spruce tips

1 tablespoon chopped goose tongue

1 teaspoon yellow mustard

Dash of paprika

Dash of Lawry's Seasoning Salt

Freshly ground black pepper

1 tablespoon prepared poppyseed, ranch, Thousand Island or French salad dressing (optional)

In a bowl, stir the mayonnaise, relish or finely chopped pickles, spruce tips, goose tongue, mustard, paprika, seasoning salt, and black pepper together. Tip: You can add a tablespoon or two of your favorite salad dressing to this tartar recipe to spice up the flavor. Refrigerate until ready to serve. Makes 1 cup.

FIREWEED DIPPING SAUCE

½ cup prepared fireweed jelly

¼ cup soy sauce

2 tablespoons sesame oil

1 tablespoon golden brown sugar

1 to 2 tablespoons cornstarch

1 to 2 tablespoons water

1 to 2 tablespoons chopped fireweed blossoms

In a saucepan, combine the jelly, soy sauce, sesame oil, and brown sugar. Set the pan over low heat and cook, stirring constantly, until the mixture is combined, about 1 minute. In a small bowl, mix

1 tablespoon cornstarch with 1 tablespoon water to make a paste. Whisk the cornstarch paste into the saucepan and stir over low to medium heat until the mixture thickens, about 1 minute. If the sauce is too thin, thicken by making a cornstarch-water paste again and stir it in. If the sauce is too thick, add a tablespoon or two of hot tap water to loosen it. Let the sauce stand for a few minutes until it's set, then stir in the fireweed blossoms. Makes ¾ cup.

SECOND FISHCAMP CYCLE

FIELD GUIDE TO FINDING HOPE

It's the spring of 2020 and somewhere between disbelief and wonder there's an uncertainty keeping you grounded like a skunk cabbage in the mud. At any moment the deer can nibble off your new spring growth or the bears can dig up your roots.

Today, my dad and I have left our hunkering-down abode to get some fresh air and look for signs of spring at Pats Lake. In the truck, it's easy to feel like things are normal, but the world now is hardly that. My dad, my husband, and I all live together at our fishcamp and we've been talking about death a lot. Not in a morbid manner, but as matter-of-fact COVID-19 talk. Would we want to be hooked up to a ventilator? Would we want to die at home? When would we want to go to the hospital? Whatever our decisions are, we will still stand on the porch listening for grouse hooting on the hillside, and still head out into the wilderness to check for bear tracks. Our favorite blueberry patch now has blossoms, and it looks like it might be a good berry year because we had snow to protect the bushes. It's comforting that some things are predictable.

My dad and I get out of the truck. My shoes squish into the mud, newly thawed from spring sunlight. The grass on the side of the road is still pale and dry, but sure enough, we spot skunk cabbage: four bright yellow tubes protrude from the muddy ditch. My dad follows me to the edge of the ditch. "Years ago, when I had my fishing boat,

I would've been fishing Back Channel by now. When the skunk cabbage comes up, the king salmon are here," he says.

As I note how many skunk cabbage plants are emerging in the muddy ditch, I consider its healing properties reflected in the Tlingit saying "your words are healing like the skunk cabbage applied to our open wounds." This moment, right here at the edge of spring, is helping get me through another day of uncertainty.

I think about the sentiment used to encourage people to stay at home during the pandemic: who are you sheltering for? For me, that answer is my dad. We were practicing social distancing by the end of February. By the first week of March, my dad was limiting his outings to stores and the post office. We haven't been doing takeout or curbside pickup. If we're in town, we're in our vehicle and we don't get out. We love to go for car rides, plus my dad and I give the local traffic report on Facebook, so we drive around town and take a photo through the windshield of our island's normal nonexistent traffic. Our groceries are delivered, and we have a drop-off location away from the house for these and package deliveries. Our daughter checks the mailbox for us at the post office because we don't go to any public place.

Farther down the road it's impassable because of snow and deep ruts, so we stop at a small muskeg. I step out and head down a narrow deer trail, past the bare alder and willow. In some places the muskeg holds my weight because it's still frozen. Despite this, a few cranberries dot the moss. I pick a handful of Labrador tea leaves. Vivian says the ideal trifecta of cold-fighting medicines is right in our backyard: s'áxt' (devil's club), gítgaa (spruce needles), and s'ikshaldéen (Labrador tea).

It's hard to live with the threat of this COVID-19 virus or even keep up with our governor's updates. Sometimes I disconnect from social media and spend a day exploring the wilderness. My daughters and I message one another updates specific to Alaska or Wrangell. In our household we check all the risk-factor boxes. My dad is an Elder and he's medically "fragile." But it's hard to think of him like that. I can remember him lifting a car out of a ditch by himself when he needed to get my stepmother to the hospital. He has stories of pulling twenty-foot lumber cants off the green chain in the sawmill and of once carrying a washing machine on his back.

I try not to dwell on our human fragility as we pass the lake again and see four large white swans and a flock of Canada geese. A goose steps gingerly on the thin ice. Spring is returning. A few weeks ago, it seemed like everything was waiting and there was a sense of impending doom. Now, the first sign of skunk cabbage, the swans, and the thawing muskeg refocus my thoughts toward promise and hope.

We drive to the end of the turnoff for the lake, and instead of heading north toward the fishcamp, we cross the main road toward the beach and the old log haul-out. Beside the road is a stretch of muskeg dotted with the red leaves of blueberry bushes, some of which are already budding. I get out and walk into the muskeg. Oscar, my border collie, follows me. I can just make out the slightly purple color of devil's club stalks beside the bushes. As I return to the truck, I note that protruding through the dry grass on the side of the road are the tiny velvet-looking leaves of Indian celery.

We head back to town. The icicles and frozen waterfalls along the bluff road are melting in the sunlight. Soon we'll have a spring landslide. It happens every year—a large boulder or two rolls out into the road. Some things we can predict and other things we can't, but mostly I think it's a wonder human beings even exist on this planet for the years we have. Our family has always taken comfort in knowing we're living here together. We're not alone. We can hunker down and shelter in place because I'm doing it for you and you're doing it for me.

What am I sheltering for? Hope. The world we will enter again—after our forced absence, after baking umpteen loaves of bread, after homeschooling our kids, after only being able to wave at our grandchildren through the window, after standing six feet or more from the possibility of hugs—will be different. I can accept that. My hope comes from seeing the skunk cabbage come up again, from watching the sandhill cranes fly in formation over my fishcamp. There the world goes again and so must I.

When I headed out into the wilderness today, I assumed I was going to look for the evidence of spring: buds and shoots, melted ice, critters and birds. But what I was really doing was looking for hope.

Skunk cabbage field in spring.

I needed reassurance. Will I be here in a couple of months? I don't know. Will my dad or my husband succumb to the virus? Will the virus hurt the people I love in communities all over Alaska? I don't know.

What I do know is that while I sit here across from my dad on our deck next to the ocean, sipping immune-boosting tea in the warm spring sunlight, rolling dice in a game of ten thousand, is that *this is it*. It is all we have. There is comfort in the change of seasons, the buds opening on the elderberry bushes, the beach grass sprouting green. And as soon as I return to considering where exactly I want my ashes spread in front of the fishcamp, the first hummingbird of the season hovers near my head and gifts the sound of her wingbeats.

PUT AN EGG ON IT AND DIP IT IN COFFEE

My dad's response to a good evening meal is typically, "This'll taste good with an egg on it," meaning "This Halibut Olympia was really good and I can hardly wait until morning to eat it with an egg on top." And he does. Often, before my dad can even comment about how good the crab enchiladas were, I say, "I know, I know. Put an egg on it!"

I stopped accepting my dad's offers to fix me breakfast at the fishcamp because I've had some strange leftovers in the omelets. I also don't like the look of leftovers with an egg on them. Go figure, because I don't like yesterday's food going to waste—I will eat devil's-club-and-black-bean salad for breakfast. I'm also accustomed to dipping just about any spruce tip sugar cookie, blueberry muffin, or salmonberry-and-spruce-tip bread into my coffee in the morning. So, our fishcamp food motto should be: Put an Egg on It and Dip It in Coffee.

Leftover halibut crepe filling? Put an egg on it. Mixed-berry hand pie? Dip it in coffee. Leftover salmon patty? Put an egg on it. Salmonberry scone? Dip it in coffee. You get it!

145

GATHERING RED SEAWEED

Since COVID-19, we've been enduring a strange world.
Whenever I need some peace, I head to the beach with my dogs.
The repetitive motion of looking down and around, of feeling cold
seaweed between my fingers, of walking carefully over slick rocks,
absorbs me into the beach world.

This morning, a spring storm has just dissipated. I'm looking
for red seaweed that may have washed up. *Palmaria mollis*, also
called ribbon seaweed or dulse, is in the phylum of the red algae,
Rhodophyta, of which there are dozens found around the world. It
grows in the lower intertidal zone in bays and exposed coastlines.
It's a reddish-brown color which makes it stand out from other
seaweeds. The fronds are narrow and grow up to ten inches long.
They typically feel leathery to the touch, or papery if it's newer
growth.

I find some and bite off a piece—it's tender and salty. As I gather
the red seaweed, I think about how spring is arriving in fits and
starts this year. One day there's a flock of robins in the grass, and
then next day, or even the same day, there's a snow squall. It's as if
Mother Nature can't decide if it's winter or spring. In Sámi culture,
this indecision is a season unto itself, one of eight: we're currently
enjoying spring-winter, or gidádálvve, which is March to April.
Gidádálvve brings more light, snow dripping from the trees, and

Red seaweed gathering at Mickey's Fishcamp.

thrushes chirping in the woods. The seasonal shift is not abrupt—it's a gradual and hopeful awakening, like a bear yawning or a robin testing the mud for warmth. Gathering seaweed is one way to enjoy this season.

Kéet sniffs my basket, curious and hoping for a snack. My border collies have been my only harvesting companions this year since the pandemic has prevented me from spending time with my grandchildren. Missing them has been the hardest thing about dealing with this virus. A new T'akdeintaan grandson named Liam arrived recently in what the Tlingit call the Underwater-Plants-Sprout-Moon. Someday, I might tell Grandson Liam we found him in a pile of seaweed. Or maybe I'll swirl a tidal tale about how his mom and I were walking the shoreline in the spring one day, and we lifted some popweed on a rock and discovered him there just like a gumboot. I told similar stories to my children—about Raven tricking Tide Woman, and about the yellow cedar log carved into the first killer whales—connecting them to their ocean culture and tideline worlds.

Depending on the tides and storms, red seaweed can be harvested from spring into summer. We've had some strong spring storms, making for good seaweed gathering. There's always something delicious washed up. Well, maybe not always. I push some popweed aside and uncover a fat worm. This type of sand worm, *Nereis vexillosa*, also called a sea nymph, likes to eat seaweed too. Without touching the strange-looking crawler, I examine it closer and consider maybe it was responsible for the mass of gelatinized eggs I found at the tideline recently. Sand worm mating swarms occur at midnight in late winter or spring. They leave behind gelatinous egg blobs too.

I stand up and continue harvesting. I walk along the seaweed patch and not twenty feet from the worm, there's a donut-shaped egg mass. I realize it could be moon snail eggs, which are normally protected inside a sand nest. The eggs were probably dislodged by the storm. Worms and eggs—it's proving to be an interesting Zen walk.

My basket is about half full of red seaweed now and I decide that's enough. If you must rinse red seaweed, only rinse it in seawater while you're down on the beach. Don't use fresh water or it'll ruin the seaweed because it washes away the natural salt and makes the seaweed limp and tasteless. Later, I'll dry the seaweed in the oven on low, because the weather most likely won't provide drier, sunny days just yet.

I head across the beach with Kéet herding me home. My cedar basket is damp with seaweed and I have relaxed. My worries have sloughed off me and are sifting down through the sand. As I walk up the stone stairs to my cabin, I consider that one night this spring, when I was checking the CDC's website for COVID-19 statistics, sand worms were swarming in mating delight, moon snail eggs were being swept away from their sand nests, red seaweed was rolling on waves toward my cabin, and Grandson Liam was being born. Life happens despite our worrying. There'll be a day, someday, when that grandson toddles on the beach with his Mummo. We can discover sand worms and fill our buckets with red seaweed. And it might happen in a season when Mother Nature can't decide if it's winter or spring.

DRIED RED SEAWEED

Dried red seaweed can be eaten as a chip like a snack, seasoned or plain. Mix dried and crushed red seaweed with other seasonings, like spruce tips or goose tongue. Add it to Halibut Olympia (a classic Alaskan dish); to fish tacos; to salmon, halibut, or crab patties; to herring egg salad; and to homemade pesto. I use it in and on almost anything I can. Red seaweed is also great fresh for stir-fries, scrambled eggs, spring rolls, soups, and fish recipes.

Gather only as much red seaweed as you'll need for a meal or two. If you're preserving it on a sunny day, then lay the seaweed out on a bedsheet on the porch in the sunshine to dry until the seaweed turns dark and crunchy.

If it's not a sunny day, preheat the oven to 250°F. Carefully lay the red seaweed out on a single layer on several baking sheets. Dry the seaweed in the oven for at least 1 hour, checking on it about every 15 minutes to make sure it doesn't burn. You can even open the oven door a bit after the oven heats up, and then turn off the oven and allow the seaweed to dry in there. Taste it; it should be crunchy like a potato chip. If the seaweed is chewy or soft, then it's not ready yet and needs a bit more time.

When the seaweed is completely dry, crumble it with your hands or use a pestle. Store in small Mason jars with holes in the lid for sprinkling, or in small sealable plastic bags, for up to a year.

A BUNCH OF HOOLIGANS

My dad and I work beside the smokehouse, our breath pluming in the morning air. The sun isn't quite up over the mountains and a light spring frost coats the prep table. My dad chops alder rounds into smaller pieces and sets a stack of wood aside. Then he kneels down in front of the smokehouse and tosses a few handfuls of alder shavings into the bottom. I consider when humans first decided to make a fire, maybe it wasn't to keep warm but to smoke fish.

As he makes a smoky fire in the base of the smokehouse, he says, "Sleeping spiders must go." I don't want to watch spiders drop from the smokehouse, so I busy myself cleaning off the table, setting up our chairs, and spraying the fish racks with oil so the fish won't stick. This morning we're smoking hooligan and I can hardly wait to taste one.

Hooligan spawn either in the lower elevations of a river or stream, or miles upstream in rivers with long, flat deltas.

We've been gifted a five-gallon bucket of Stikine River hooligan. The hooligan gift economy thrives in Wrangell—boats go upriver, "river rats" set nets, and they bring home buckets of hooligan. The call goes out on phones by text and on Facebook, at the grocery store checkout stand, down at the harbors, over coffee and cream shrimp on toast. *Do you want some hooligan?*

With a hose, my dad fills the tote half full of water. He opens a box of canning salt and pours it into the tote and stirs, explaining to me how we don't need as much salt as we do for salmon because the fish are smaller and less fatty. He stirs the brine until the salt dissolves, then pours the bucket of hooligan into the brine and stirs around the fish.

Hooligan eggs are "broadcast" (spread) over sandy river bottoms by the females, then fertilized by the males.

If someone referred to a Wrangellite as a "hooligan," we wouldn't see it as a bad thing at all. During his short stint as Wrangell's sheriff, Wyatt Earp allegedly said Wrangell was wilder than Tombstone. Maybe we are a bit wilder since we live and thrive in the Stikine wilderness area. Actually, hooligan is our name for eulachon—*Thaleichthys pacificus*—candlefish, saak (Lingít), ooligan, or oolichan. Hooligan are smelt about ten inches or less in length. They're silver-blue in color while in the ocean, and turn grayish-brownish-green in the fresh water.

Hooligan eggs are coated with a sticky substance so they can attach to sand particles or pebbles.

Wrangell's hooligan run occurs about mid-April. When the migratory birds return and the sea lions gather, the hooligan arrive. Hooligan are different from salmon in that hooligan don't always return to their home stream but to the streams in the area with the most favorable conditions. Sea lions, whales, salmon, ravens, crows, and bears all get excited for the return of the hooligan, and fishermen head up the river in their scows with their nets.

Now, my dad and I pour the tote full of fish and salted water into a filter system my dad invented for this process. The fish quickly drain. I stand next to the table as he scoops hooligan onto each rack. I arrange them close to each other but not touching. Next, my dad builds a small, tented fire in the smokehouse. He knows how hot to make it and how much smoke is needed to smoke hooligan.

Newly constructed smokehouse at Mickey's Fishcamp, Wrangell, Alaska,
built by Mickey Prescott.

*Female hooligan can lay up to thirty thousand eggs. Depending on the
water temperature in the rivers and streams, hooligan eggs hatch in
twenty-one to forty days.*

Smoke curls from the vents in the top front of the smokehouse
and drifts across the small road behind the trees. Crows alight in the
nearby trees above us and squawk, trying to convince us they're a

part of the gifting culture, which they are, and reminding us they're ready for a morsel to drop on the ground.

Hooligan connects us to place, fills us with river silt, and brushes us with cottonwood scent. We are smoked fish, grease, milt, eggs, and river sand. Smoked hooligan is part of me, our town, and our community—Wrangell hooligan are an essential part of our island's gift economy. There's even a Hooligan Reading Fair at Evergreen Elementary School. If you check a Wrangellite's DNA, you'll probably find we are a percentage hooligan.

The Stikine River current carries newly hatched hooligan from fresh water to the ocean where they feed on copepod larvae, plankton, and krill. After three to six years at sea, hooligan return to spawn and die.

After the fish are finished smoking, we remove the racks from the smokehouse and carefully take the hooligan off. We take the smoked fish into the kitchen and the house fills with a wonderful scent.

When Grandson Jonah comes to the fishcamp to visit, we try to get him to eat a fish, but he doesn't want to.

"You can light them like a candle," my dad says. "Really. It's pretty neat." He turns to me and adds, "I did this for you when you were a kid." My dad takes the small fish, pierces it with a wooden skewer, and balances the fish across the top of a glass jar so the fish's head is poking up through the mouth of the jar and the tail is facing the bottom. He lights it and the hooligan catches fire, burning like a candle. Jonah leans in to examine it.

I say, "Pretty cool, huh?"

Jonah smiles. It is cool.

As the flame rises, I say to Grandson Jonah, "See, it's a candlefish. Saak, in Lingít, like a sock you put on your foot."

"Saak. Saak," Jonah repeats.

Grandson Jonah doesn't want to try to bite the head off the fish. I don't pressure him. Someday he might try it.

River and stream temperatures affect the timing of spawning migration, and the water conditions and ocean survival contribute to the varied hooligan returns.

I bite into a piece of smoked hooligan and I am five years old again, eating it for the first time. I watch as my older sister puts a hooligan's head in her mouth. She isn't making a face or spitting it out. She says, "Mmm. Good." With encouragement from my Grandpa Al, she eats the whole thing. My grandfather hands me a smoked hooligan. I take the fish in my small hands. I put the fish head end in my mouth and bite. It's crunchy and salty like a potato chip. It's good. I eat the whole crispy fish, savoring the crunchy tail.

I pick up another smoked hooligan, bite the off the salty head and eat it, bones and guts and all. Even the tail.

SMOKED HOOLIGAN FRESH SPRING ROLLS

MAKES 10 SPRING ROLLS

These fresh rolls celebrate spring in Wrangell. The taste of hooligan brings back great memories for me. Smoked hooligan can safely be eaten whole: head, bones, guts, skin, and tail. You can stuff these rolls with anything you like, including zucchini, avocado, and seasonal beach greens. Leftover vegetables can be used in a bowl of ramen.

1 (13-ounce) package thin rice noodles

FOR THE THIMBLEBERRY OR BLUEBERRY DIPPING SAUCE:

½ cup water

¼ cup soy sauce, plus more if needed

2 tablespoons prepared hoisin sauce or additional soy sauce

1 teaspoon sesame oil

½ cup mashed thimbleberries or blueberries with their juice (or substitute jelly or jam)

3 tablespoons firmly packed brown sugar, or to taste

3 tablespoons cornstarch

FOR THE SPRING ROLLS:

Spring roll rice wrappers

6 smoked whole hooligan, flaked (or substitute any smoked or unsmoked cooked fish)

1 English cucumber, cut into matchsticks

1 large carrot, cut into matchsticks

1 red, orange, or yellow bell pepper, cut into matchsticks

1 cup purple or green cabbage, shredded or cut finely

1 cup chopped sea lettuce, or other seaweed

3 green onions, chopped

1 handful fresh cilantro, chopped

Put the rice noodles in a shallow bowl of warm water and soak them until softened, about 30 minutes. Once softened, drain the noodles in a colander.

To make the Dipping Sauce, in a small saucepan over low heat, mix the water, soy sauce, hoisin sauce, if using, and sesame oil. Drain the mashed berries, reserving the juice in a separate small bowl, and add the berries to the pan. Add the brown sugar 1 tablespoon at a time to sweeten the sauce to your taste.

While the mixture warms, add water to the bowl with the berry juice to make ½ cup total of liquid. Mix in the cornstarch with a fork. Gradually pour the cornstarch mixture into the warm sauce mixture in the pan and stir. Increase the heat to medium and stir until the sauce thickens, about 30 seconds. If the sauce is too thick, add more soy sauce or water until the desired consistency is reached. Keep warm. (If you're making the sauce ahead of time, warm it up for dipping the rolls prior to the meal. Add a tablespoon or two of water and stir it over low heat until warmed through.) Transfer a few tablespoons of the dipping sauce to a small dish.

To assemble the Spring Rolls, first fill a round glass or metal pie plate with very warm, almost hot, water. Dip a spring roll wrapper in the water, then remove it as soon as it softens and changes texture. This only takes a few seconds. (The paper can become gummy if you leave it in too long, so it's best to wet one wrapper at a time and roll up the spring roll before starting on another.) If the water cools, dump out the cool water and add more warm water.

Put the soaked wrapper on a plate or cutting board. Fill each wrapper with a small handful of each ingredient in this order (remember, you will be making 10 rolls): rice noodles, flaked hooligan, a teaspoon of dipping sauce, then the vegetables—cucumber, carrot, bell pepper, cabbage, sea lettuce, green onions, and cilantro. Fill just below the halfway point on the wrapper, in the center. Don't put too much filling and leave some room on each side of the wrapper.

Fold the sides of the wrapper over the filling toward the center to resemble an envelope. Then roll up the end of the wrapper closest to you, rolling away from your body. Set the roll on waxed or parchment paper on a baking sheet. Repeat to soak, fill, and roll the remaining wrappers with filling. Serve immediately with the remaining dipping sauce. Extra rolls can be wrapped and refrigerated for a couple days.

CARRYING ON TRADITIONS

My youngest daughter, Nikka, Cháas' Koowú Tláa, didn't let the pandemic stop her from harvesting spruce tips, one of her favorite foods and an important part of her Tlingit culture. For Nikka, harvesting spruce tips is about teaching her children about respect, the ways and values of her ancestors, and the medicinal and nutritional value of plants. Nikka has been harvesting spruce tips for food for the last decade. She recalls walking through the woods as a child while spruce tips were budding. "I'd pick a couple and eat them as I explored the woods. Some were sweet, some were citrusy, and some tasted woodsy, meaning they were too big to be picked. It was fun to pick the needles off to eat the tart center as a refreshing snack."

Harvesting during a pandemic means there's less help from extended family and friends who are sheltering in place or keeping their social groups small. "Some days it's hard to make myself go out and get things like spruce tips. I'm used to my mom and my grandpa saying they're ready to go. It motivates me to get out there with them," Nikka says. If you're committed to keeping a safe distance from others, it can be difficult to find areas that aren't frequented by other harvesters, especially closer to town. If you want to avoid the crowds, harvesting in the wilderness, especially in smaller groups, can be tough. "It's challenging to find a safe spot where I can stay near my car in case unfriendly wildlife show up," Nikka says. Fewer family members also means less talking and singing, which lets wildlife know you're in the area.

This year, Nikka and her partner John are harvesting with their seven-year-old, Jonah, and one-year-old, Grandson Bear. Nikka says that adjusting her spruce tip–picking schedule to the baby's schedule pretty much goes like this: "Feed the baby, put him in the front pack or stroller depending on where we are, pick spruce tips, baby wakes up and I feed him again, play with him, then pick more spruce tips and feed the baby again, and finally get one last pick in for the day." It takes more time, but she says it's doable.

These problems don't take away from the satisfaction of having a good batch of spruce tips to put up for the year. Nikka makes all kinds of foods from spruce tips, but her favorite is making a jelly of spruce tip and fireweed. She's also been making candy with spruce tips and especially loves spruce tip water and spruce tip tea. "It's a refreshing water that tastes just how the tips smell. I love adding in lemon slices."

Many of the things Nikka knows about spruce tip harvesting she learned from family. She says, "I look for the brown husks starting to fall off and I know it's time to start picking. I like to get a variety: from small tips to ones that're almost too big. When I'm cooking with them, I like the flavor of the different stages all mixed together. When I pluck one to eat, though, I look for a tip with the needles closed and pressed together. Those have the best flavor." Experiential, hands-on learning is an important part of Tlingit education and Nikka is hoping the pandemic won't stop people from passing on Traditional Knowledge. "Picking spruce tips and using them in different ways is something we need to pass on to the next generation. I'm afraid the knowledge will be lost, and people won't pick them anymore if we don't take the time to harvest even in difficult times."

Nikka believes it's important to harvest with family, especially Elders. "I always learn something from my Elders. When you go as a family, it's a different level of respect you're giving to the land and the plants. When a grandmother or grandfather is showing kids how to pick, and what not to pick and why, there's a deep connection

Jonah Hurst and little brother James "Bear" Hurst learning to harvest spruce tips.

happening. It's respectful to our ancestors. It's teaching my kids how to be good parents and good grandparents or uncles one day."

Harvesting with family and Clan has always been a part of traditional healing and we need to stay as healthy as we can. Getting outdoors heals many things, a value embedded in the Tlingit culture. Nikka says, "I love harvesting spruce tips. It makes me feel connected to the earth and when I show the plants respect by being careful when picking, only taking so much from each tree, and saying thank you, the trees feel that respect and will continue to produce tips."

Nikka is sad her grandpa and I can't go harvesting with her this year, but she understands. Dad and I are keeping a close-knit unit to avoid being exposed to COVID-19.

Since the pandemic began, young families like Nikka's have faced many challenges including homeschooling, lack of work, and finding jobs that won't endanger the family through exposure. Things that were once simple now take more thought and planning—even getting out to buy groceries and run errands is challenging. Nikka says *time* is also one of the obstacles to harvesting. "With a seven-year-old and a one-year-old, by the time I get out to pick, more than half the day is gone. I try to keep the kids interested so they don't feel it's something they have to do rather than something they want to do. Some days, though, I have to make them go with me and get it done because every day is another day closer to the end of spruce tip season. Spruce tips don't wait for you, so I have to just get out there and do it!"

Nikka explains that her son Jonah goes through the same process every year where he doesn't want to go picking but wants the jelly, so he ends up tagging along but not helping. "But this year he's older so he's been walking around with a bag, harvesting spruce tips anywhere he goes! He's excited about what we're going to make with them."

Someday Nikka will be back out harvesting with her extended family again. For now, she has great memories to think on. "About four years ago, I was spruce tip picking with my mom and my son Jonah who was three at the time. The weather was beautiful and the tips were ready. Jonah was being good, so we picked and picked until we poked ourselves too many times and our hands hurt. We took a lunch break with a beautiful view of Zimovia Strait. It was a perfect Southeast Alaska day."

For Nikka, the best part about spruce tip picking is sharing them with the local Tribe. Every year she brings the foods she makes with spruce tips to share with Elders and those who can't harvest any longer. "I love teaching my sons to take care of their Elders, even ones they don't know!"

Nikka's connection to Tlingit Aaní is sustained through harvesting spruce tips. "My connection to the land when harvesting is hard to explain. Time kind of stops or slows down. Everything is quiet except the birds. If I listen carefully, I can hear our ancestors saying gunalchéesh for carrying on our traditions."

FIRST TASTE OF SPRUCE TIPS

If you've never tried spruce tips before, here are two simple ways to have your first taste of the forest. Go pick a few spruce tips in the spring and try them in a comforting hot cereal or sprinkled on toast. These are perfect ways to get guests or kids to try spruce tips for the first time.

SPRUCE TIP OATMEAL

Cook whole or quick oats according to the package directions. Chop 3 to 4 spruce tips, or more for a bolder flavor. Sprinkle the chopped spruce tips over the oatmeal and then add milk and brown sugar, honey, or spruce tip sugar (chopped spruce tips mixed and dried in sugar) to taste. Take a bite. If desired, add more chopped spruce tips. Serve warm.

SPRUCE TIP TOAST

Toast some bread and finely chop 2 fresh or frozen spruce tips. Butter the toast and sprinkle on a bit of sugar, then top with the chopped spruce tips. Enjoy!

THE ART OF SALMON

My dad sits at the long plastic table outside near the smokehouse with a small block of cedar in front of him, slicing off thin, pencil-like pieces. While we're smoking salmon, he's making cedar pegs, a long-lost salmon fishing tool. Once the peg is inserted into the herring, the herring is bent to mimic a wounded herring flashing silver. My dad claims salmon like the scent of cedar. He's caught a lot of salmon in his lifetime, so I believe him.

There's an art to knowing salmon and your fishing gear. My dad caught two big king salmon yesterday, so today we're sitting near the smokehouse on lawn chairs, watching the alder smoke curl up from the vents, making cedar pegs, and telling stories. The Sámi way of storytelling is to tell many stories at once, one story leading to another and another.

My dad caught his first big king salmon at the age of nine, when he was out trolling with his dad one morning. "I had gone out from my dad's boat in a nine-foot skiff—a wooden rowboat with no motor," he remembers. "I was rowing it along the beach, hand-trolling with a blueberry branch and a line with a wooden plug that looked like a blueback-herring for bait. I trolled along the shore, and *boom!*—a fish started pulling me around, out toward the straits. I let him fight until he got tired—I had enough sense to know you have to tire a big salmon out or it'll wear you out—and when the skiff finally stopped

Mickey Prescott gives a thumbs-up after a good day of fishing
in front of Mickey's Fishcamp.

moving, I pulled the line in. He didn't have much life left in him after fighting, but I couldn't pull him in because I was so little and he was so big, so I tied him up to a little cleat on the back of the skiff. I rowed back over to my dad's big boat and he helped me land it. It was a big fifty-pound king salmon!"

My dad learned to fish salmon from his dad, my grandfather, who learned many of his fishing techniques from the Tlingit and Scandinavian fishermen he knew. In my dad's elderly years, his life is filled with salmon memories. The stories and lessons are as varied as fish jumps, but they all teach me to be a better salmon fisherman. There's an art to the bend in the herring, to knowing which fish jumps in front of the fishcamp.

My dad shares his knowledge: "You can tell by the jumps if the fish is a king salmon. Kings jump all the way out with a big splash, usually one to three jumps at a time. Cohos jump clear out of the water too, but they don't jump as many times, usually a single jump or two. The sockeye are easy to spot because they jump three or four times in a circle. They look like skipping a rock—we call them skippin'-rock sockeyes. The sockeyes also slide on their sides partway and their tails stay in the water. The humpy flips. He jumps a single jump with a smaller splash. In a big school, the humpies jump all over the place. And the dog salmon, they jump, but not as much. They come to the surface and do a lot of finning. You watch for finners besides the jump. Diving dogs, we call them. They go down under a seine net to avoid being caught."

From fishing salmon around the islands his whole life, my dad can also tell where the salmon are from and where they were headed based on their behavior. He tells me a hatchery fish will stay down and fight, like a cross between a halibut and a salmon, while a Stikine River king salmon will come up to the surface fast. "Bradfield kings fight a lot," he says. "They are short and stocky and bigger than the Stikine River kings, who are longer and narrower. An Aaron's Crick king has an emerald-green back instead of a bluish one—there's no mistaking them. Ocean-run kings are heavily bright like a herring and are good fighters." Appearances are telling too. "Ocean kings are always red. I've never gotten a white one out there. Usually, you get more white winter kings than red because there's less krill for them to feed on."

I marvel at this knowledge and wonder if I'll remember everything. My dad gets up from his chair and checks the smokehouse fire. He adds another alder log and it starts smoking good. He sits back down at the table and I ask him about "choking a herring," a term I've heard my whole life. My dad says it's a troller-fishing term used in the old days, a technique he learned from his dad. "People don't know how to do that anymore," he says. "The hook you use when you choke a herring is different from a normal hook; it has a flat shank rather than round. When I was about nine years old, I'd sit on the boat during the bad days and make the cedar pegs for him. You use cedar pegs when you choke a herring."

Holding up a cedar peg in his hands, he shows me what he is talking about, his fingers forming a hook and an imaginary line. "With the hook and line, you come up through the gill flap and come out by the eye, and then down around the head, jaw, and gill flap area. Then with the hook you go through the opposite eye and come out through the other eye. It makes a stitch around the head and mouth. Then insert the hook into the body, right behind the gill flap, and bend the herring. You feed the hook as far as you can toward the tail.

Then you bring the back of the hook out of the body into the curve. If you have slack, tighten the slack. Insert the herring peg through the opposite eye following the backbone until it almost pokes out."

He makes a snapping motion with both hands. "Then break off the end of the herring peg. Cedar breaks when the fish strikes."

I get up to check on the salmon in the smokehouse. Smoke pours out once I open the door, and I wait a little for it to clear before I look over the racks. "Looks good," I say. "About another hour." I go back to my chair and sit down. We are quiet for a few minutes, comfortable in the silence.

"What about Lil' Joes?" I finally ask. A few years ago he made me a Lil' Joe: a trolling plug.

"I taught myself how to make Lil' Joes," he says. "That's what the manufacturer called them. It's a plastic commercial trolling plug. Those things are hot right under the surface—the big Bradfield kings go nuts for them. Only down two fathoms. I couldn't find any more plastic ones and there was no internet then, and no one carried them locally, so I decided I could make them for nothing. I carved Lil' Joes from red cedar and painted them."

As the smoke wafts up through the hemlock branches and the spruce trees, we laugh at the noisy crows who've discovered we're smoking fish today. We talk over them. My dad gets up and goes into the nearby shed and brings out a brightly colored gaff hook on a long stick he uses for landing fish. He hands it to me. "I took an old gaff hook and dressed it up a bit."

As he shows me his gaff hook—where he wrapped line around it then put some newfangled rubber paint on it—he starts to tell a story. "My old gaff was pretty good. I had it for years. I was pulling up cohos like a bugger and I went to bonk the fish, but I misjudged my swing distance and strength, and when I brought my arm back, I stuck that hook between my eyes. Talk about a headache. All those years I'd been gaffing fish. I looked like someone had shot me with a .22 between the eyes."

"Jeez," I say, laughing, holding the sharp gaff. "It's a wonder you survived." Now, I'll remember not to bonk myself. I'm sure glad my dad made it this far, through a life teeming with stories, to this full smokehouse so he could teach me the art of salmon.

FISHCAMP SALMON TACOS

MAKES 8 TO 15 TACOS, OR 6 SERVINGS

I love salmon tacos. There are a few steps to making them, but they're worth it. Make your salsa first so the flavors can blend. Of course, you can use purchased corn or flour tortillas, but homemade tortillas are extra special. I've included two tortilla recipes here because I love both kinds, and adding spruce tips makes them Alaska special. If you like, construct your tacos with a corn tortilla inside a flour tortilla for a tasty combination. I like to arrange the toppings in small separate bowls at the table for guests to serve themselves.

FOR THE BLUEBERRY SALSA:

1 cup fresh or frozen and thawed blueberries

1 jalapeño chile, diced

¼ cup diced red or yellow onion

½ cup diced red bell pepper

½ cup diced green or yellow bell pepper

¼ cup chopped fresh cilantro

2 tablespoons chopped goose tongue (optional)

1 tablespoon chopped spruce tips (optional)

Pinch of garlic powder

1 lime

FOR THE CORN-SPRUCE TIP TORTILLAS:

1¾ cups masa harina, plus more if needed

2 to 3 tablespoons chopped spruce tips

1 cup hot water, plus more if needed

1 tablespoon Spruce Tip Juice (page 20)

FOR THE FLOUR-SPRUCE TIP TORTILLAS:

2½ cups all-purpose flour, plus more for shaping

1 tablespoon chopped spruce tips

1 teaspoon baking powder

½ teaspoon Spruce Tip Salt (page 20)

4 tablespoons melted unsalted butter, or ¼ cup avocado oil.

¾ to 1 cup hot water

2 tablespoons Spruce Tip Juice (page 20)

Canola oil, if desired

FOR THE SALMON TACO FILLING:

1 large salmon fillet, about 2 pounds (preferably king salmon, but coho is okay)

Salt

Freshly ground black pepper

Squeeze of fresh lemon juice

Sprinkle of ground cumin

FOR THE TOPPINGS:

¼ cup chopped goose tongue

2 cups shredded green cabbage (or locally harvested greens)

1 cup shredded white cheddar, yellow cheddar, or Pepper Jack cheese

2 Roma tomatoes, chopped

½ cup chopped or sliced black olives

½ cup plain yogurt or sour cream

To make the Blueberry Salsa, in a bowl, combine the blueberries, jalapeño, onion, peppers, and cilantro and mix well. Toss in the goose tongue and spruce tips, if using. Sprinkle with the garlic powder. Squeeze the juice from the lime into the salsa and mix in gently. This salsa keeps in the fridge for a few days.

To make the Corn–Spruce Tip Tortillas, in a large bowl, mix together the dry masa harina and the chopped spruce tips. Measure 1 cup of hot water and stir in the Spruce Tip Juice. Slowly add the Spruce Tip Juice–hot water mixture to the dry masa and mix, adding just enough additional hot water to make a ball of dough. The dough should be soft but not sticky; add more water or masa harina if it's too dry or too wet. Cover the bowl with plastic wrap and let the dough rest for 30 minutes.

Divide the dough evenly into 15 small balls and cover them with a damp towel so they don't dry out while you're cooking. Flatten the dough balls with either a rolling pin or a tortilla press.

If using a rolling pin, place each dough ball between two sheets of plastic wrap or waxed paper and then roll the dough into thin, round tortillas. If your dough dries out, add a sprinkle of hot water. If the dough sticks to the plastic wrap, add a tad bit more masa. Stack the formed tortillas on a plate or tray with wax paper or plastic wrap in between each tortilla until you're ready to cook them.

If using a tortilla press, open the press and put a small square of plastic wrap over the bottom plate. Put a dough ball in the center and cover with another square of plastic wrap. Before you close the press, press down gently on the ball with your hand to flatten the dough a bit. Now close the top plate and press down firmly with the handle. Open and turn the tortilla ninety degrees, then close the plate and gently press the handle again to make sure the tortilla is thin. Open the press and peel off the top piece of plastic wrap, then flip the tortilla onto your hand with the dough side down. Gently peel off the plastic wrap on the other side. Stack the tortillas on a plate or tray with waxed paper or plastic wrap in between each tortilla until you're ready to cook them.

Warm a large cast-iron pan over medium-high heat. Add a tortilla and cook for about 60 seconds on the first side, then flip the tortilla and cook for 60 seconds more or until small brown spots form. Stack the cooked tortillas on a plate under a clean dishtowel to keep warm or store them in the fridge and reheat them before using.

To make the Flour–Spruce Tip Tortillas, in a large bowl, stir together the flour, chopped spruce tips, baking powder, and Spruce Tip Salt. Stir in the melted butter with a fork, creating a crumbly texture. In a separate bowl, add 1 cup of hot water and the Spruce Tip Juice. Using a wooden spoon, slowly add just enough hot water infused with Spruce Tip Juice into the flour mixture until a dough forms. Transfer the dough to a lightly floured work surface and knead into a soft ball. The dough should be soft but not sticky, so add more water or flour as needed. Cover the dough with plastic wrap and let it rest for 30 minutes.

Divide the dough evenly into 8 balls. On a lightly floured surface using a floured rolling pin, roll out each dough ball into an 8-inch round. Stack the tortillas on a plate or tray with waxed paper or plastic wrap in between each one until you're ready to cook them.

Warm a cast-iron pan over medium-high heat. Add a tortilla to the pan and cook until small brown spots appear, about 30 seconds, then flip and cook the other side until the tortilla starts to puff up and brown spots appear on the underside. You can cook the tortillas in an ungreased pan, though sometimes I put a tiny drop or two of oil in the pan and rub it around with a paper towel to keep the tortillas from sticking. Stack the cooked tortillas on a plate under a clean dishtowel to keep warm or store them in the fridge and reheat them before using.

To make the Salmon Taco Filling, preheat the oven to 400°F. Season the salmon with salt, pepper, and a squeeze of lemon and place it in a baking dish. Bake until the flesh turns opaque and it flakes easily with a fork. This should take about 10 minutes per inch of thickness. For example, a 2-inch-thick fillet might take 20 minutes.

Use a fork to flake the salmon into a bowl and remove any errant bones. Sprinkle a bit of cumin on top.

Set out the toppings: goose tongue, cabbage, cheese, tomatoes, olives, and yogurt or sour cream.

Assemble each taco by spooning the salmon filling into a tortilla, adding the toppings of your choice, and finishing with a spoonful of Blueberry Salsa.

THE TREAT BENEATH YOUR FEET

I stand on my porch in my hoodie looking over the beach below. I'm hopeful. Last night's wind might've brought seaweed right to my door.

I look at my border collies, Oscar and Kéet, and say, "Beach." They rush to the porch gate. I open it and they run toward the stone stairs, romping down the steps to the beach. I stop at the top and they look up at me expectantly. *Is it time to play the stick-toss game?* they seem to be asking.

I go down the stairs to the beach. I walk a few feet along the sand, sit on a large rock at the bottom of the seawall, and remove my shoes. Kéet drops a stick at my feet, hopeful. She barks and I shush her, though bald eagles have already screeched the neighborhood awake. It's 6 a.m., the tide is out, and I'm going sea lettuce harvesting.

Sea lettuce is not the kind of lettuce you buy in the grocery store or grow in your garden, but it certainly looks like that. Sea lettuce is a seaweed, in the genus called ulva. It's edible and I love it. Although I've eaten popweed and dried black seaweed most of my life, I'm enjoying learning more about other types of seaweeds.

Sea lettuce fronds are fragile; the seaweed will fall apart when rubbed between your fingers. As a harvester, I pick and pack it very gently. The fronds can be as small as six inches and grow as large as two feet. There are nearly one hundred different types of sea lettuce found on beaches around the world. Some look so much alike, even scientists have trouble telling them apart without looking at them through a microscope. There are several types of sea lettuce in Southeast Alaska and scientists are still making changes to their names.

I stand up from the rock and step on the sand with my bare feet. Despite the fact it's summer in Southeast Alaska, the seaweed is wet and cool. I step carefully, like a heron walking across the beach. The crows have already been turning over the seaweed and picking bugs between barnacled rocks. A half dozen gulls float in the water at the tide's edge.

Sea lettuce thrives in the intertidal zone, the area where the ocean meets the land between high and low tides. It loves the Inside Passage's sheltered bays rather than shores where there is lots of wave action. It's often ripped from rocks in storms. For sea lettuce, it's all about balance. Nora Dauenhauer, my Lingít language instructor and mentor, taught me that balance is an important concept in the Tlingit culture: there is balance between the moieties, in Northwest Coast art, in harvesting from the land and sea, in ceremonies, etc. Harvesting sea lettuce is one way to teach balance to the next generation. Too much wind and rain can batter the delicate seaweed. Too much sun can cause it to rot.

Some fronds of sea lettuce are about the size of a big dinner plate, while others are the size of your hand. Sea lettuce is commonly dotted with small holes. I often find its bright green fronds entangled in stranded popweed at the tideline. If you're new to seaweed gathering, sea lettuce can be easily missed; it looks thin and wilted and is often mistaken for a tissue on the beach, especially once it starts to turn pale and die. But sea lettuce are nutrient scavengers, which means it can grow well in polluted areas. For this reason, make sure there aren't any septic tanks, sewer outfalls, or dump sites in the area where you harvest. Be careful to find a historically clean site because sea lettuce can be contaminated with toxic heavy metals still found in old industrial sites. Know your neighborhood.

I walk through the popweed, bending to pick up a large frond of bright green lettuce. It's so thin and delicate I can see my hand underneath. Sea lettuce appears unappetizing to many who have

Author walks barefoot in the seaweed while collecting sea lettuce.

never tried it, but it's tasty and good for you. It's known to help with weight loss and maintaining or lowering blood sugar. A wet frond across the skin soothes a sunburn. You can eat it raw: chop it up fresh and add it to soups, salads, spring rolls, or ramen. Some types of sea lettuce are fried to make seaweed chips. I prefer it dried and used as a seasoning; it's one of the main seasonings I use on fish and meats, in soups, and on eggs. It can even be a replacement for salt in some recipes.

Sea lettuce is connected to rocks with a tiny holdfast so small you can barely see it. Some harvesters use scissors or a small knife and cut the sea lettuce off the rocks at the base of the holdfast. Others, like me, harvest the detached sea lettuce from the tideline. I sometimes take a basket with me to collect it, while other times I just drape the fronds on my forearm or pack it piled high in my hands.

Sea lettuce is shared by limpets and tiny snails. I pick or rinse off the critters and return them to the beach. In this barnacled world among seaweeds that are good for you, it's hard to imagine an abnormal sea lettuce bloom can kill you. There's a species of sea lettuce that spawns huge blooms called "green tides"; when the seaweed dies it gives off a gas—hydrogen sulfide—that can kill humans. The blooms are thought to be caused by runoff from agricultural areas and overfertilized rural and urban sites.

Back at the fishcamp, I carefully lay out the bright green fronds on my picnic table in the sun. Some people use a sheet to dry it on. Sometimes I drape strands over my porch railing. Because we live in a rainforest, sometimes I dry the sea lettuce on baking sheets in a sunlit window or in the oven on a low temperature. When the seaweed crisps up, I crumble it with my hands and put it in a small Mason jar with holes in the lid. Putting dried sea lettuce in small individual baggies works too.

Walk, search, bend, gather. Harvesting sea lettuce is meditative whether I walk barefoot or not. I take notice of things: a piece of driftwood shaped like a bird, a new patch of arrowgrass growing up nearby. The sand fleas are hopping along with me, and my basket is full of dripping sea lettuce.

DRIED SEA LETTUCE

Dried sea lettuce is a versatile Alaska kitchen staple. I like to use fresh sea lettuce in fish recipes, soups, and stir-fries, but I love dried sea lettuce for seasoning. Try it on salmon or halibut, in soups, and in egg dishes. You can also use it to season steaks, chicken, macaroni and potato salads, fish patties, or spring rolls.

Head to the beach and harvest at least 4 cups of sea lettuce. When you get home, lay out the fronds in a single layer on baking sheets. If it's a sunny, hot, dry day, bring it outside to dry.

If it's not a sunny day, preheat the oven to 250°F. Dry the sea lettuce on the baking sheets in the oven for 15 minutes, flip the fronds over with a spatula, and continue drying in the oven until the seaweed looks dry, about 30 minutes. Remove from the oven and let cool on the baking sheets.

Once the seaweed is crisp and dry, crumble the seaweed with your hands, then carefully store the flakes into sealable plastic bags or a Mason jar for up to a year. You can poke holes in the Mason jar lid so you can sprinkle the seaweed on your food.

MUSKEG LOVE

I walk along the logging road, searching the roadside for small red berries I call lowbush cranberries. My dad and I are prepared; having scoped out this muskeg for huckleberries on a previous expedition, we discovered some unripe cranberries. We'll pick them now because it's after the first frost. Today is a perfect fall day: cloudy and mild. When wearing rain pants, boots, a raincoat, and a hat, I prefer it not to be sunny.

I stand on the side of the road, figuring out the best path across the small ditch into the muskeg. I remember a story my dad once told me about a young doctor new to Wrangell who went hiking in the muskeg behind town and never came back. Locals went looking for him, but he had disappeared without a trace. Some of the holes and ponds seem bottomless and to have claimed unwary souls.

I step into the bog. I love the wide-open spaces of larger muskegs like this one. Oscar jumps across, making his way deftly through the muskeg, sniffing everything. My dad remains at the edge, picking the cranberries there. I'm harvesting two types of cranberries. Some harvesters differentiate between the two, but I call them both lowbush cranberries, despite the fact they're two different plants often growing near each other. Bog cranberries, *Vaccinium oxycoccos*, are slightly larger berries and grow along the moss, with each berry connected to the plant by a single, thin, threadlike stem. Lingonberries, *Vaccinium vitis-idaea*, also called mountain cranberries, are smaller berries that grow on a tiny evergreen plant with as many as five or six berries on one stem. They're both tarter and higher in vitamin C than store-bought cranberries.

I walk out into the open muskeg. I'm wearing a bright yellow vest over my raincoat as it's hunting season. In the larger bogs I can keep an eye out for critters who might be curious about me. Hairy rhizomes, creeping stems, twisted tree trunks, drooping cones, and scaly, gray-barked trees flourish around me. Muskeg life is wet, mushy, juicy, fleshy, tangy, glabrous, globose, and glandular. The bog is prickly and sticky; plants catch bugs to devour them, and deep, dark ponds catch humans and animals. Despite the danger, I love it all.

With each step my boots squish down into the bog. Muskegs are fragile. Off-road vehicles, too many harvesters, and even footsteps can scar a landscape. Muskeg reminds me of a giant, live sponge, or a large blanket or rug. In summer, muskegs are dotted with white and pink flowers, grasses, tea, bull pines draped in usnea, and lichen-covered stones. In the fall, they are dressed in bright reds, golds, and browns.

I wind my way around the holes and ponds. My rain pants swish when I walk. I inhale the delicious scents of muskeg life and head to the spot I had previously located. There is a sense of danger, a mix of continuous life and death that defines the muskeg. Things can kill you here. Not only do you have to be careful about stepping into a hole or meeting a large, hairy animal, you also need to know the difference between edible Labrador tea and poisonous bog rosemary and bog kalmia. These poisonous plants are cousins of laurel, azalea, and rhododendron, and they all contain toxins.

In the fall, the bog rosemary and bog kalmia look similar to Labrador tea (Hudson Bay tea), having lost their blossoms and grown to full height. But if you ingest the poisonous plants, you can expect lots of horrid progressive symptoms: watery eyes, nose, and mouth; loss of energy; slowing pulse; vomiting; dropping blood pressure; irregular breathing. You'll get drowsy and lose your coordination. Finally, you'll become paralyzed and die. Yikes!

I kneel in the squishy muskeg near a small pond. A cold, wet sensation seeps in despite my wearing rain pants. The pond is so dark I can't see down into it. It must be deep. Surrounding the pond is a band of black muck where cranberries are growing in the soaked earth. After telling Oscar not to get too close to the pond, he sits down beside me.

Already my feet and knees are leaving an impression in the muskeg. I set my berry bucket next to the hole and start picking, being careful not to get too close to the fragile embankment. In my mind I hear another of my dad's muskeg stories:

I was in my late teens going trapping, hiking across the muskeg behind town. I had on my winter clothes and gear: boots, snowshoes, and a hundred pounds of traps. In the muskeg I stepped on a pond of ice about ten feet across and started walking. It wasn't thick enough to hold me in the middle. I went through.

I went in up to my chest and my snowshoes locked tight down into the water and muck. There was only a small bull pine nearby and I couldn't reach it. I had my arms out. I did a side dive and reached down and undid each snowshoe and put the shoes up on the ice surrounding me. I rolled out onto the thicker ice. That was the end of trapping for the day. I learned the hard way.

Oscar gets up and wanders back and forth between my dad and me, checking on our berry-picking progress and sniffing game trails. After a bit, the patch is picked, though I have left some berries for the critters. I move to the side on my knees, reaching for the moss, looking for hidden berries. I find another patch on a small knoll of red moss. Oscar plops down right in the middle of the patch. "Gee, thanks, Oscar," I say to him. Two rifle shots echo in the distance. Oscar barks. Occasionally he sniffs the air. I listen for his warning growl and scan the muskeg. Though berry picking is meditative, you must stay aware of your surroundings.

The muskeg is my happy place, my thinking and contemplating place. It's good medicine. There is something about being down on the wet earth, reaching my hands into it, that connects me to the land. The muskeg is one big medicine blanket. My daughter Vivian taught me this. Beneath my feet are treatments for warts, indigestion, rashes, migraines, ulcers, coughs, diabetes, UTIs, fevers, and fever blisters. Some plants stop hemorrhaging and

Oscar and Kéet explore the muskeg with the author and her father
while keeping a lookout and listen for bears and wolves.

other ones are effective against streptococcus, staphylococcus, and pneumococcus. There are also treatments for anxiety and intestinal worms—not necessarily together.

I think of this as I stand up. My knees are stiff, and my hands ache from the wet and cold. My bucket is half full, but that's enough for today. Oscar follows me back through the dying cottongrass, around the lichen-covered stones, and back to the road. Again and again I breathe deep, inhaling the muskeg scent. I turn and look behind me. Impressions of my feet are pressed into the bog as if a ghost has just walked there. I imagine the muskeg slowly, ever so slowly, rising up to fill my space.

MUSKEG MUFFINS

MAKES 12 MUFFINS

There's nothing more beautiful and scented than a Southeast Alaskan muskeg. I wanted to create a muffin that reminded me of all the wonderful and interesting plants growing there. I make these muffins using plants and berries I've harvested throughout the year and then stored in sealable plastic bags in the freezer: chopped or whole fireweed blossoms, spruce tips, Labrador tea. You can use just cranberries, just blueberries, or a mix of both berries in this recipe. I like both in my muskeg muffins.

1 large egg

¾ cup almond–coconut blend milk (or substitute whole milk)

¼ cup avocado oil

¼ cup Spruce Tip Juice (page 20)

1 tablespoon yogurt or mayonnaise

2 cups all-purpose flour

½ cup firmly packed golden brown sugar

3 tablespoons flaxseed meal

2 teaspoons baking powder

2 tablespoons fireweed blossoms or pulp

1 tablespoon finely chopped Labrador tea

1 tablespoon finely chopped spruce tips or spruce tip pulp

½ cup pine nuts

¼ cup whole muskeg cranberries or chopped purchased cranberries (or substitute Lingonberries)

½ cup fresh or frozen blueberries

FOR THE MUSKEG STREUSEL TOPPING:

¼ cup all-purpose flour

¼ cup firmly packed golden brown sugar

½ teaspoon finely chopped spruce tips

½ teaspoon finely chopped Labrador tea

2 tablespoons unsalted butter, room temperature

To make the muffins, preheat the oven to 400°F. Line a 12-cup muffin pan with paper cups, or grease only the bottoms of the cups with an oil-coated paper towel, then dust with flour.

In a bowl, using a fork or whisk, mix together the egg, milk, oil, Spruce Tip Juice, and yogurt. In another bowl, mix together the flour, brown sugar, flaxseed meal, baking powder, fireweed, Labrador tea, and chopped spruce tips. Using a large wooden spoon, mix the flour mixture into the egg-milk mixture until just combined. It will have lumps, but that's okay. Then gently fold in the pine nuts and the berries, being careful not to overmix. Fill each muffin cup with the batter, dividing evenly; the cups should be a little over half full.

To make the Muskeg Streusel Topping, in a bowl, mix together the flour, brown sugar, spruce tips, and Labrador tea. Add the butter and, using a fork or your fingers, mix until crumbly. Sprinkle the topping evenly over the batter in the muffin cups.

Bake until muffin tops are golden brown, 20 to 25 minutes. Place the muffin pan on a wire rack to cool for a few minutes before removing the muffins. Serve warm for breakfast, lunches, and coffee time.

GIFTS FROM THE PORCUPINE

Being killed by wolves, dying on a trail, being run over by a truck: these are the ways porcupines gift me their quills. North American porcupines, *Erethizon dorsatum*, are plentiful on Wrangell Island. I've never hunted nor eaten a porcupine, but people tell me they're delicious. The traditional way of harvesting quills from a live porcupine requires tossing a blanket onto the back of the porcupine; when the porcupine crawls out from under the blanket, quills are stuck to the fabric.

I explain these harvesting details to Grandsons Timothy and Jackson. They've come over to the fishcamp to help me harvest porcupine quills from a dead porcupine.

Porcupines are found throughout most of the forested areas of Alaska, although they're not found on Prince of Wales Island in Southeast Alaska and neighboring islands to the west.

I hand Timothy and Jackson safety glasses and gloves for the process. I place the dead porcupine out on a table covered with paper bags. "We have to thank the porcupine," I say. "Gunalchéesh, porcupine." They repeat after me. I thanked the porcupine when I'd first discovered it in the forest too. I recall kneeling in the wet soil near the roots of a tree and thanking the beautiful creature before I put its carcass into a bag.

Porcupines can live up to thirty years, unless...

"How did it die?" Grandson Jackson asks.

"Great-grandpa Mickey says probably a wolf," I say. I turn the porcupine over. The underbelly is nearly gone, as if a wolf or another carnivore had turned it over to eat it. "These underside hairs aren't prickly, but they can help the porcupine climb trees." We examine the porcupine's big, long hairs and thick, muscular tail. Porcupines use their tails for climbing and for defense.

"Speaking of trees, have you heard the story about Porcupine and Beaver?" I tell them the story from their Tlingit culture about the origins of the striations on the bark of the hemlock tree, which has everything to do with a porcupine and a beaver, a story filled with ecological Traditional Knowledge.

As I'm telling the story, I show my grandsons how to pull off the quills. Timothy tugs gently with the pliers and a quill comes off. Jackson does the same. We pile the quills on a paper plate.

"Xalak'ách' is the Tlingit word for porcupine," I say. It sounds like xuth-uck-UCH, but not quite. Jackson tries the word. Timothy doesn't say anything. I encourage him and he tries it. It sounds pretty good.

We continue pulling quills with our gloved hands using small pliers. There are several tried-and-true quill-harvesting methods. Some people gently press pool noodles or towels against the quills. My harvesting mentor, Dr. Dolly Garza, recalls, "My sister and I would drive around the back loop in Juneau with an old foamy pillow and whack dead porcupines to get the quills from them." Others tack up the animal's hide and press a knife to the skin while pulling the quill out gently.

Artists categorize the quills into four types: large and thick, long and thin, fine, and extra thin. The large, thick quills from the tail are used to cover large areas in quill embroidery, on pipes and handle work, and for fringes. For loomed quillwork, artists use the long, thin quills found on the porcupine's back. Fine neck quills are ideal for embroidery, and the really thin quills near the belly are used in line quilling. In Tlingit Traditional Knowledge, specific quills are perfect for earrings. The larger quills, k'ishataaganí, make great

At Mickey's Fishcamp, Timothy and Jackson Pearson help
harvest porcupine quills from a dead porcupine.

earrings. X̱aawú is the general word for porcupine's hair or quills.

My grandsons and I don't save the long hairs because this porcupine has been dead for a while and is rather stinky. But people do harvest the long hairs for making headdresses, masks, and jewelry, plus other artful things. I use porcupine quills for my mixed media sculptures; quills have adorned my sea pottery flowers, a giant moon's eye, and a porcupine woman. *Porcupine Woman* is my mixed-media sculpture collaged with sea pottery shards with floral patterns on them that I found on our old garbage dump beach. The model for *Porcupine Woman* is my great-niece Maleah, and the sculpture is covered in about a hundred quills and includes an earring made by Maleah. Maleah also makes jewelry from quills to pay for any extra expenses at Dartmouth College.

Several crows land in the nearby alders and caw. They must smell the carrion. "Is it a boy or a girl?" Jackson asks.

"I don't know," I say. Not much remains of its underside. And I don't know its age. "Did you know a male porcupine splashes the female porcupine with pee—you know, urine—if he wants to mate? And if she's not ready, she shakes off the pee and leaves."

The boys laugh.

Porcupines only have one baby, called a porcupette, a year.
The gestation period is around 210 days, or seven months.

Quills are usually cleaned after harvesting, but not always. Quill artists often use hot, soapy water to soak and clean the quills until they are bright white. Removing the oils makes them easier to dye while bleaching can damage the quills, making them brittle. I only rinse mine off because I don't intend to dye them.

"Guess how many quills are on an average porcupine?" I ask my grandsons. "This is a small porcupine, but guess."

Timothy guesses fifty thousand. Jackson guesses five thousand.

"Thirty thousand!" I say. "That's a lot."

Grandson Timothy looks a bit concerned at this number.

"Don't worry, we won't be harvesting all of them," I say. "Only as many as we can."

We continue working on the quills. I take off my gloves and pull a large fat quill with my bare fingers. I hold it up. "Tap it gently," I tell them as they each pull off a glove. I hold the barb up and they each touch it with their fingertips. "Each quill has about eight hundred barbs near the tip."

To protect the mother porcupine, a porcupette is born in
a thin placental sac, which tears by itself soon after birth.

We talk story and pull quills for another hour, until their attention spans wane. We fill several containers with quills and sort through them, picking out any hairs.

"Well," I finally say, "I think we got most of the thirty thousand quills."

Baby porcupines are born with their eyes open, covered with long hair and soft quills. About an hour after birth, the soft quills dry and harden to protect the baby.

I lean over the porcupine. "Someday your quills are going to be dangling on someone's ears or decorating art on a wall." I tuck my hair over one of my ears to show my grandsons the rainbow-colored beaded porcupine quill earrings that Maleah made me. I flick the quills with my finger and my gift from a porcupine dances above my shoulders in the afternoon light.

SPRUCE TIP CHOCOLATE BROWNIES

MAKES 24 SMALL BROWNIES (OR 15 LARGE)

After the hard work of harvesting porcupine quills, eating these brownies is perfect. And, of course, I tell the grandkids there are the spruce tree's "quills" in them.

1⅓ cups all-purpose flour

2 cups firmly packed golden brown sugar, or 1 cup white sugar and 1 cup golden brown sugar

¾ cup unsweetened cocoa powder

1 teaspoon baking powder

3 to 4 tablespoons finely chopped fresh or frozen spruce tips, plus more for sprinkling (optional)

⅔ cup avocado oil or melted butter

4 large eggs

1 teaspoon vanilla extract

1 teaspoon Spruce Tip Juice (page 20)

½ cup chopped walnuts or pecans (optional)

Preheat the oven to 350°F. Grease and flour a 9-by-13-inch baking pan and set aside.

In a large bowl, combine the flour, brown sugar, cocoa, baking powder, and spruce tips and stir well. If using frozen spruce tips, chop them first and then pat dry with a paper towel so that they mix with the dry ingredients better.

In another bowl, beat the oil, eggs, vanilla, and Spruce Tip Juice with an electric mixer until well blended, 1 to 2 minutes. Add the egg mixture to the flour–spruce tip mixture and stir with a wooden spoon or rubber spatula just until blended, being careful not to overmix. If you're adding nuts, gently fold them in.

Pour the batter into the prepared pan, spreading it evenly. Sprinkle the extra chopped spruce tips on top if you like a stronger spruce tip flavor. Bake until a toothpick inserted into the center comes out clean, 20 to 25 minutes. The brownies will slightly pull away from the pan. Let cool on a wire rack.

Cut the cooled brownie into 24 small or 15 large squares, then dive in!

IT'S THE LITTLE FISH IN LIFE: RAINBOW SMELT

My dad rolls the small fish in beaten egg and then flour, and sets it in the hot frying pan beside three other smelt. He stands over the stove, explaining how he used to catch smelt for his friends the Urata family. He wants me to try the fish, but he doesn't know what kind of smelt they are. He supposed they wintered in the harbor; all he knows is they aren't hooligan.

At Mickey's Fishcamp, we're all about a sustainable, subsistence life. These are Western catchwords for what my daughter Vivian calls, "Haa atx̱aayí haa k̲usteeyíx̱ sitee"—Our food is our way of life. I'm learning food gathering and teaching it to my children and grandchildren, so I wanted to know about this bright little fish. I'm used to seeing smelt—their small, silver glints in the harbor's green water have been a memory flashing throughout my whole life—but for a long time I'd assumed they were herring.

I stack a few plates on the counter and go outside on the porch. In a bucket, a couple dozen fish glint silver. My husband had set out a herring net in the harbor overnight hoping to catch herring, but all he had ended up with was a small bucket of smelt. *What kind of smelt?* I wonder. I tap the search engine on my iPhone, looking for information on various smelts in Southeast Alaska. Rainbow smelt are about eight inches long and have an olive-green spine. They have brightly colored scales and a small adipose fin. They are distinguished from other smelt by their protruding jaw with teeth on the tongue. *Really?* I pick one up, open its mouth, and scrape my fingertip over its tongue. Teeth! I bring the fish inside to show my dad. I hold the fish, mouth open. "It's a rainbow smelt! Feel the tongue." He sticks his finger inside the smelt's mouth and agrees.

The smell of hot oil and fish fills the small kitchen. My dad flips the smelt on the pan. "You can tell when hooligan or smelt have arrived in the spring because the birds, Western grebes, sit in a long line out in the strait feeding on them. They've done that as long as I can remember," he says. He tells me he once caught a king salmon with a rainbow smelt in its stomach. He had never seen a king that had eaten one, but the smelt were in the harbor then. "I knew where that king had been."

When it comes to fish and fishing, my dad is the expert on king salmon. We sometimes refer to him jokingly as "the king of kings." He says when the hooligan are schooling up in deeper water, getting ready for the ice to come out of the Stikine River, that's when the rainbow smelt show up in the harbor. Information on rainbow smelt in Southeast Alaska is slim. I did learn the fish are anadromous, a word I love because it sounds like an erotic star map. It means the fish live part of their lives in the ocean and the other part in fresh water. Rainbow smelt hatch in freshwater streams and live about two to six years in the ocean before returning home to spawn. Hatchlings eat crustaceans, other tiny creatures' eggs, water fleas, zooplankton, and algae. Adult rainbow smelt subsist on small shrimp, squid, sea worms, crabs, crustaceans, and other small fish, including their own species.

My dad turns off the burner and declares lunch is ready. I put two smelt on my plate and sit down at the table. "Turn the fish like this," my dad instructs me, turning the fish on its belly, backbone upward. "Press down with your fork." I do as he says and the meat on each side separates. I lift the tiny backbone and set it aside. The white flesh is light and delicious.

One of the reasons I like living at the fishcamp is I get to learn about things I don't know and experiment with fishing and harvesting. I learn rainbow smelt have a superpower called macromolecular antifreeze, meaning they accumulate glycerol and

Mickey Prescott and a bucketful of rainbow smelt.

antifreeze proteins in their bodies. Frogs have similar capabilities, but unlike frogs, rainbow smelt use their abilities in the ocean, overwintering in estuaries beneath the ice. Amazingly, rainbow smelt haven't been widely studied in Southeast Alaska. Later, I ask my older sister why we didn't eat rainbow smelt as kids. She tells me we were king salmon snobs, meaning since we were a family who fished for our food, in addition to fishing commercially, we had all the fish we could eat and didn't need rainbow smelt. Plus, my grandfather often supplied us with hooligan (saak, eulachon, or candlefish), the better-known smelt.

My family now knows what rainbow smelt are and what they taste like, yet we still have questions, so I ask Wrangellites on our local community Facebook page about rainbow smelt. A Tlingit fisherman says they're a winter fish and he looks forward to eating them when other fish aren't available. Why didn't I know this? Like most Wrangellites, we're hooligan connoisseurs, but rainbow smelt? Half the respondents don't know what rainbow smelt are, and if they do, they don't harvest them regularly. Some confuse rainbow smelt with hooligan. Several people harvest rainbow smelt in the spring.

Another fisherman says smoked rainbow smelt is a favorite of his. As far as catching them, fishermen use either a herring net or a herring jig.

My dad likes to write information in his tide book. He keeps track of the weather, water temperature, and even how we prepared different fish. He likes keeping notes so he can open the book and say, "Last year we got a bucket of rainbow smelt with a herring net." He remembers harvesting smelt in the late fall and early winter, but we are still learning the rainbow smelt's ways. We know rainbow smelt are sensitive to light, temperature changes, and rapid currents. That explains why they are found in the calm harbors. Will we find rainbow smelt year round or only in the spring, and in which harbors and on which beaches can we fish for them? My dad will write down these answers when we figure them out.

What we do know is the rainbow smelt's biggest threat to its future: humans. Overharvesting for personal or commercial use can jeopardize the health of this little fish. When we catch smelt, we are careful. This year I want to try smoking rainbow smelt, teaching my grandchildren as I learn how. Harvesting this little fish from the sea has become part of our way of life here at the fishcamp. "Haa atxaayí haa ḵusteeyíx̱ sitee," I tell myself. Our food is our way of life. I will teach my grandchildren that phrase and its meaning too.

FRIED RAINBOW SMELT
(HOW DAD DOES IT)

SERVINGS VARY

*Five or six smelt per person is just right, so get as
many fish as you need. If you don't have rainbow smelt,
you can substitute hooligan or herring.*

FOR EACH SERVING:
Frying oil (like canola oil)
2 eggs, beaten
1 cup powdered pancake mix

5 to 6 smelts, gutted and cleaned
Lawry's or Johnny's Seasoning Salt
to taste
Tartar sauce for serving, if desired

Pour ¼ cup oil in a medium to large frying pan so that there's a thin layer of oil and set over medium heat. While the pan is heating, beat the eggs with a fork in a shallow dish. Put the pancake mix in another shallow dish. When the oil is hot, roll each fish in the egg and then the pancake mix, then carefully place in the hot oil and sprinkle with the seasoning salt. Brown the fish in the hot oil until the tails are crispy, 2 to 3 minutes per side. Drain the fish on a paper towel-lined plate.

To serve, put the cooked fish belly-side down on the plate with the back upward, then press on the spine. The meat will fall off the backbone. Eat the meat plain or dipped in tartar sauce.

THE BUNCHBERRY YOIK

My dad, Kéet, and I survey our surroundings: bull pines and spruce draped with lichen, a soggy muskeg, and bright reddish-orange berries contrasting with green leaves dotting the roadside. Cornus unalaschkensis: I call them bunchberries, and in the Lingít language, k̲'eikax̲étl'k. They're one of my favorite fall berries.

I've come here to a special spot on the island to pick bunchberries and reflect on how I can chant their song. With a handful of other students from around the world, I'm taking a yoiking class online from Sámi instructors Elin Kaven and Jungle Svonni from Sápmi in Norway. A yoik (or joik, in Scandinavian languages) is a Sámi chant. The practice of yoiking is somewhere between singing and throat singing. A yoik uses the tongue to manipulate the sounds and sounds are produced farther back in the throat.

I've been practicing traditional and contemporary yoiks for a couple of months. I even practiced an old reindeer-herding yoik. My instructors want us to compose or sing our first yoik and said we should pick something we love when we're ready. I love bunchberries, so maybe I can "fetch" their yoik, since yoiks are already in everything and we just need to fetch a yoik when we want to hear it.

I sit down on the ground surrounded by bunchberries. Kéet

sniffs the area. My dad walks the road edge, scoping out more berry patches. The surrounding carpet of bunchberries reminds me of a fairyland, which is fitting because my ancestors learned to yoik from the fairy people.

My dad walks back toward me, gesturing with his cane. He's spotted a big patch down an embankment. I plunk a handful of berries into the bucket. "Didn't we call these snakeberries?" I ask my dad. "Or soapberries?" I'd heard those names as a kid, but I'm pretty sure we mixed them up.

The Alaskan bunchberry, *Cornus unalaschkensis*, is a dwarf species of dogwood that trails along the ground and up tree trunks. Also called trailing dogwood, coastal bunchberry, and western bunchberry, it ranges from Alaska, British Columbia, Washington, Oregon, and California to the far north including the Canadian Arctic and Greenland. Bunchberry flowers look like one single flower, but they're actually a cluster of tiny flowers surrounded by four petal-like bracts—leaves growing from a flower's axis. I've learned our bunchberry is often confused with *Cornus canadensis*, another species of dwarf dogwood from the East Coast. Supposedly it's easier to tell the difference when they're flowering, as *unalaschkensis* has a slightly purple tinge to the bracts while *canadensis* bracts have a green tinge. They both flower in the late spring and early summer. Their berries, growing in the center of the flower, are pale red-orange at first and eventually turn bright red.

Bunchberries are a favorite of photographers. In spring and summer, their white blossoms carpet roadsides and forest floors and rim the muskegs. Later, their bright red berries contrast with their vibrant green leaves, resembling festive winter holiday decorations. In the fall, the leaves turn a beautiful purple. Yes, they're photogenic, but what I like best is you can still find bunchberries to eat in October. They're a beautiful way to bid goodbye to the berry season.

"Bunchberries," my dad says. "Yes, and snakeberries and soapberries."

Bunchberries have a foamy, tasty pulp inside and a crunchy seed. Some people assume they're poisonous or don't care for the taste, but they're one of my favorite berries. They are also a favorite food of songbirds and birds migrating south for the winter. People use the leaves for deer calls by placing them on their tongues, pressing the leaf to the roof of the mouth, and blowing; plus, there are medicinal uses.

I stand up and walk toward the location my dad spotted and make my way down the embankment. Kéet scampers downhill to join me, and my dad heads to the other side of the road to inspect the groundcover for berries. This place, the same spot where I harvest hanging lichen, has always made me feel like I should be singing something and I never knew why. Sámi yoiking has its origins in nature, giving a voice to it and honoring it. As I'm learning, there's a difference between a song as we understand it and a yoik. A song is *about* something or someone, and a yoik *is* that something. A yoik is the energy or essence of that thing, so a bunchberry yoik I create will not be *about* bunchberries—it will *be* bunchberries.

I lean against the dirt embankment, pick a few berries, and taste them. They pick easily since you can grab more than one berry at a time. As I pick, I start to sing, making small, upbeat sounds. I use the northern Sámi sounds, called syllables. Sounds, not words, are the most important tools for yoikers. Yoiks are natural parts of everyday life, like picking berries and petting the dog. Yoiks are often impulsive, arising when the spirit of nature moves the chanter. They're used in storytelling, lullabies, memorials, and ceremonies. They are chanted for relatives and friends, for children, or at special sites or events.

I pick the berries on the hillside then turn and make way toward an old stump where more berries cascade like jewels. Bunchberries love the rainforest and thrive on decaying material like stumps. The old stump is like a grandmother, with her grandchildren berries surrounding her. She nurtures them. That would be a good sense of the yoik. Now I consider: should I fetch a yoik from the berries themselves, the old stump, or the berry-picking event? You use a low tone like *na* or *te* to fetch the yoik from the earth. I'm probably going about this song practice the wrong way, though, because the yoik comes to you. A yoik has no beginning and no ending.

Between my dad and me, we pick half a bucketful of bunchberries. It's almost time to go. Now, what to do with them when we get home? I can make jam or jelly, or muffins, perhaps. Some people combine them with other berries in recipes because bunchberries have a lot of pectin and they help set up jams and pies. Maybe I'll just eat them and sing them. I'm thinking about what I've been learning in the yoik class. If you start with yoiking something you love and are familiar with, you'll have a deeper understanding and connection with what you're yoiking. I love bunchberries and yoiks. Learning more about both is fascinating and good for the spirit.

Whether the yoik is an animal, place, nature, person, event, or ceremony, it evokes the characteristics, energy, and personality of what is yoiked. Nature yoiks capture the energy of golden devil's club leaves and the splash of a November storm against my seawall. So what's the personality and characteristic of a bunchberry? My instructors said we should pretend to be what we're yoiking. I have to pretend to be a bunchberry. Bunchberries evoke my childhood. Bunchberries provide energy for humans and birds. To compose a yoik for a thing, you use your hand to find the notes in the shape of the thing you want to yoik. A cluster of happy, red, round berries might resemble shorter notes bunched together: *na la-lo la-lo ng, la-lo la-lo ng*. I can see the bunchberries in my yoik and feel the yoik in my feet. Before I climb out of the muskeg and up onto the road, I grab a few more bunchberries and put them in my mouth. *Na la-lo la-lo ng, la-lo la-lo ng, la-lo la-lo ng, la-lo la-lo ng.* This is the beginning of a bunchberry yoik and perhaps it was already there waiting for me, bright and tasty.

MIXED ALASKAN BERRY HAND PIES

MAKES 12 HAND PIES

Pies that fit in your hand go everywhere the Alaskan adventurer goes: fishing, hiking, camping, or harvesting in the forest. They're the perfect snack! Make the piecrust and filling ahead of time so that when you're ready to bake, it's just a matter of rolling out dough and filling it. I like using ½ cup each bunchberries, salmonberries, blueberries, and thimbleberries.

FOR THE PIECRUST:

2 cups all-purpose flour
¼ cup sugar
Pinch of salt
8 tablespoons (1 stick) frozen butter, cut into small chunks
1 egg yolk, beaten
4 to 8 tablespoons ice-cold water

FOR THE BERRY FILLING:

2 cups mixed Alaskan berries or other fresh berry mix
¼ cup sugar
Pinch of nutmeg and/or cinnamon (optional)
1 to 2 tablespoons cornstarch
1 teaspoon lemon juice or Spruce Tip Juice (page 20) (optional)

1 egg white, beaten
Sugar or finely chopped spruce tips for sprinkling

To make the Piecrust, pour the flour, sugar, and salt into a food processor and pulse twice. Add the frozen butter cubes and pulse a few times until a crumbly texture forms and the butter is broken down to the size of peas. Mix the beaten egg yolk with 4 tablespoons of the cold water (but not the ice) and slowly add the mixture 1 tablespoon at a time to the dry ingredients, pulsing once or twice after each addition until a dry, crumbly mix forms and and sticks together when you press it between your fingers. Add more cold water if needed.

Turn out the dough onto a lightly floured work surface. Pat the dough with your hands until it comes together. Form it into a flat disk and cover it with plastic wrap. Refrigerate for at least 1 hour.

To make the Berry Filling, in a small saucepan, combine the berries and sugar. Add the nutmeg and/or cinnamon, if using. Use a fork or potato masher to break down the berries a bit; you don't want to mash the berries too much, because the less liquid the better. Spoon out 4 tablespoons of the berry juice and place in a small bowl, mix the berry juice with the cornstarch, then set aside. This will be used later to thicken the berry mixture.

Place the berries over low heat and bring to a simmer. Simmer for about 5 minutes, stirring occasionally. Whisk in the juice-cornstarch mixture and stir until thickened, about 2 minutes. Add lemon or Spruce Tip Juice for added flavor, if using. Remove the pan from the heat and let cool.

When ready to bake, preheat the oven to 375°F and line a baking sheet with parchment paper. On a lightly floured surface, roll out the dough to ⅛-inch thickness. Use a jar or biscuit cutter to cut out 12 circles. Try not to overhandle the dough to preserve the flaky layers.

Spoon 1 to 2 tablespoons of filling in the center of a dough circle. Don't overfill or it'll ooze out the sides. Brush the dough edges with the beaten egg white. Fold the edge over to make a semi-circle then crimp the edges with a fork or your fingers to seal in the filling. Repeat until all 12 dough circles are filled. Place the formed pies on the prepared baking sheet. With a sharp knife, cut two or three small slits in the pie tops. Brush the tops of the hand pies with the beaten egg white and sprinkle with sugar or spruce tips.

Bake the pies until golden, about 25 minutes. Let cool on a wire rack before serving.

LUNGS OF THE ISLAND

My dad and I drive up a dirt hill, the ocean to the right and muskeg (peat bog) to the left. Around us the tall spruce and old bull pines are heavily dressed in thick, hanging lichen. As we crest the hill, the breeze sways the lichen like waving hair. The road splits at the top, curving to the right to a narrow pull-through road that meets again with the main road. Between the main road and the pull-through is a bowl that dips down and is filled with a small forest of trees and berry bushes.

"This place is the lungs of the island," my dad says. "The air is really clean up here."

Wrangell Island is shaped like a snow goose flying toward the Stikine River flats, with its beak touching the river and its wings outstretched. Since the nearby flats are a resting area for huge flocks of migrating snow geese, the description fits. Our fishcamp is located in the crook of the snow goose's neck, and the "lungs of the island" are right where the goose's lungs would be, near Nemo Point.

My dad parks the truck and we get out. He walks around on the road as my dog Oscar and I head down the embankment into the forested bowl between the pull-through and the main road. I breathe in deeply and Oscar sniffs the bushes. I start to walk through the trees to examine the yellowish thick, hanging threads of what I've called "moss" my whole life, which is not actually moss but lichen.

Hanging lichens grow where the air is clean. But what kind of lichen is growing in the lungs of the island? Is it old man's beard or what some call angel hair? Hanging lichens are hard to tell apart, especially from a distance. Vivian says when she's harvesting a certain type of moss or lichen, she finds a sample she's sure of and puts it in her pocket so she has something to compare.

It's easy to get hundreds of types of moss and lichens confused. In Southeast Alaska, though, you most often see two common hanging lichens: *Usnea longissima*, which hangs in long green-gray strands from old trees (hence the name old man's beard), and *Alectoria sarmentosa*, which also hangs on trees but is shorter, bunchier, and more yellow-green (angel hair).

Many of the English names for both these hanging lichens are used interchangeably. It turns out what I thought was old man's beard is really angel hair (which is also called deer moss and witch's hair). I'm still learning, but I think I've got this right. Old man's beard is also called usnea (in Lingít, séixwani) and can grow up to twenty feet long. The lichen in the lungs of the island is not nearly that long.

As I walk through the forest, I'm mindful of my daughter's harvesting rules: harvest windblown lichen from the ground or from the broken branches that have fallen from the tree; only take a small amount from each spot; carefully remove the lichen or use scissors to cut it from the branches and don't break them. We are not the only ones who live here—deer browse on the lichen, especially in winter, and birds use it for building their nests. I use lichen for my art projects, but with today's harvest I plan to learn how to make tea from the medicinal lichens and my daughter is going to make antifungal medicine.

I consider how hard my daughter works at harvesting and making medicines from lichens and plants. Historically, colonizers discouraged this practice in many places around the world, including Tlingit Aaní and Sápmi, our Sámi homeland in Scandinavia. In Sápmi, Traditional Practitioners, and even those seeking the healing properties of plants, were criminalized. Colonizers associated the natural world with a demonic or savage world. A century ago, this activity I'm doing now, harvesting lichen, would have been illegal.

Usnea tea.

The lichen I pull from a branch is clumpy and has no long chain at its center. What I'm holding is *Alectoria sarmentosa*—angel hair. Both it and old man's beard contain usnic acid, yet angel hair lichen is not classified in the genus *Usnea* because it lacks this long center chain. I put some lichen in the red cedar basket I'm carrying and continue on.

As I make my way through the small forest, past the bare blueberry bushes and with the dirt road at eye level, I feel as if I'm in an undersea world. My boots sink into the muskeg and lichen strands wave in my face around me. I consider how the ocean is growing on our trees, because angel hair and old man's beard are actually a fusion between an alga and a fungus functioning together as a single organism. I can see this as I look around.

I find lichen in this area on both live and dead trees. There's a misconception that the lichen kills the trees, but lichen and elder trees have a special relationship. The hanging lichen finds a good place to grow in the arms of the elder tree, and in turn, the elder tree cleans the air. Hanging lichens are used as environmental indicators, or bioindicators, because they're extremely sensitive to sulfur dioxide pollution. If lichens are present, it shows the air is clean. In different parts of the world, hanging lichens are known by other names: seaweed of the mountain, spirit of the north wind, air grass, and excrement of air.

Many already know the about the secret of lichens. Components such as usnic acid in these two specific hanging lichens are commonly used in both commercial products and traditional medicines as treatments for fever, pain, UTIs, yeast infections, kidney and bladder infections, coughs, sore throats, skin lesions and cuts, bug bites, and athlete's foot. They are also used as ingredients in sunscreen, toothpaste, deodorant, dyes, and more.

As I make my way into the basin, the trees get denser. There's nothing like being knee-deep in young, fragrant yellow cedar and hanging lichen. I stand within inches of the hanging lichen and closely examine the strands. It's definitely not what we call old man's beard but angel hair. But since angel hair lichen, despite containing similar medicinal qualities, is not categorized in the *Usnea* family, when we say we're "going out to harvest usnea," we should be harvesting the longer, chainlike old man's beard.

I'm still figuring out the differences between just two types of lichen. There are fifteen species within the genus *Usnea* in Alaska and more than five hundred species of lichens overall, so I've got some learning to do. If I had all the time in the world, I'd be learning every one of Southeast Alaska's lichens and mosses. I don't have that kind of time, though I think it's a good goal. Before my dog and I climb back up out of the bowl, I stop in the middle of the trees. With my basketful of lichen around my neck, I inhale and breathe in the lungs of the island.

USNEA TEA

MAKES 2 CUPS

Immunity-boosting usnea tea tastes slightly earthy. The tea has many benefits, but the most common is it helps relieve indigestion, soothes a sore throat, and supports the metabolic process, meaning it helps you maintain a healthy weight. It's anti-inflammatory and anti-fungal too. Old man's beard contains usnic acid. If you're pregnant, breastfeeding, or taking prescription medicines, always consult your doctor before trying any traditional medicines or teas.

2 cups boiling water

2 cups old man's beard (*Usnea longissimi*)

Honey, for flavoring (optional)

In a clean 2-quart pot, pour the boiling water over the old man's beard. Let steep for 30 minutes, then strain out the solids. Serve in a cup, adding honey to taste.

Alternative method: Put 2 cups water along with the old man's beard in a small pot, and simmer for 30 minutes on very low heat. The Tlingit traditionally pour ¼ cup of the steeped water into a serving cup and then add more hot water and honey to flavor the tea.

HIGHBUSH CRANBERRIES AND TRADITIONAL VALUES

September sunlight glints on the lily pads dotting the surface of Pats Lake. I stand along the lakeshore with my daughters, my grandchildren, and border collie Kéet. We are out scouting for highbush cranberries. Berry picking for us is a family event with several generations harvesting together. In the Sámi worldview, many teachings come from nature and family Elders, and education is experiential.

Pats Lake is my children's traditional subsistence area and where we pass on harvesting and gathering knowledge. I'm still learning about *Viburnum edule*, the scientific name for highbush cranberry (in Lingít, kaxwéix). The fruit's not a true cranberry, but we Southeast Alaskans call it that. Highbush cranberries ripen in late summer and early fall, but after the first frost they start to get a strong musky scent and fall off the branches. Some say the berries smell like stinky socks, but I'd describe them more like earthy cranberries. Highbush cranberries are easiest to pick right before the frost.

By harvesting from Pats Lake, we celebrate this land, our family and traditions, and the recent successful effort by our community and our Tribe to protect the Pats Creek Valley from the storage and disposal of lead-contaminated soil from a local junkyard. In my children's and grandchildren's Lingít language,

Timothy Pearson (author's grandson), Mickey Prescott (author's father),
and Jackson Pearson (author's grandson) harvest berries at their
favorite family berry-picking spot.

they say, "A káx̱ yan aydél wé tl'átgi"—We are stewards of the air
land and sea—and in my Sámi culture, we say, "Nature reflects
the Creator." From nature we get many of our teachings. Picking
highbush cranberries at Pats Lake with my daughters and grandkids
provides the opportunity to pass down these cultural values to the
next generation.

Highbush cranberry blooms in May through July, and the new
berry turns yellowish and ripens to bright red in late August or early
September. Highbush cranberries are firm at first, then they soften
and eventually fall off the bush. Some stragglers will stay on the
bush all winter, though, and be food for birds and deer. The plumper
later fruit has less pectin in it, so some gatherers harvest when the
berries first turn red. They have flat seeds that are not usually eaten.

My instructions to my grandkids for today's expedition: wear
boots and a raincoat, and follow directions. We gather at a grassy
marsh near a picnic table. My grandkids grab berry buckets from
my car. We use recycled plastic coffee cans, ones their great-grandpa
fashioned with a thick string. We spot a few bushes and set out, but

first we announce we're in the area by saying, "Grandfather, it's just us." In the Sámi worldview, as well as in Finnish and Tlingit, it's disrespectful to say the name "bear" out loud in the woods. I adhere to this and teach it to my grandchildren. Yelling "ho, bear" or "hey, bear" could call the bear to you.

As we head into the marsh I say, "Watch your footing. Consider each step. Especially if there's no game trail to follow."

Highbush cranberry bushes don't have many leaves, but they can grow up to twelve feet high. The berries grow in small clumps and the leaves turn a beautiful red-orange in the fall. When bright red, the berries resemble ornaments on a Christmas tree. Now, cranberries hang high above my grandchildren's heads. I show my grandchildren how to gently pull the branches down. If you're too rough, the berries fall and the branches break. As we're picking, we say, "Gunalchéesh. Thank you."

I help my grandchildren climb up on a stump, making sure their footing is secure to reach a tall bush. I let them each try a cranberry but warn about the tartness. They make faces. Yes, they're tart, but they're high in antioxidants. The Oxygen Radical Absorbance Capacity (ORAC) scale measures a food's antioxidant activity, and a score above 40 ORAC is high and fresh. Highbush cranberries score 174. They're also high in vitamin A, vitamin C, and fiber. We're going to make ketchup out of them, some jelly, and maybe fruit leather. You can even make traditional medicines from highbush cranberry leaves and bark. Medicinal uses include treatments for infections, sore throats, and constipation.

"These berries are an important fall and winter food for birds like grouse," I say, "so make sure you don't pick all of them in one area. Leave some for the birds. And if you spill your bucket, leave them for the critters who scamper on the ground."

My grandchildren and daughters are set up to pick the berries here, but I spot tall branches across the road, beyond a stand of big spruce trees, that might be highbush cranberries. The waist- to head-high grass and the marshy lakeshore will make it difficult to get to them. Highbush grow well within the tall grass along the perimeter of marshy areas. They also like the rocky slopes along the edges of logging roads. From a distance, highbush resemble alder and crabapple, so you can get really excited only to learn it's a young alder. I decide I'm going to check it out.

I carefully step on the rocky embankment leading down into the grass. I trudge over rotting skunk cabbage and pass by a few game trails. Kéet follows me, and within minutes she's soaked. I make my way beyond the stand of trees. With each step I listen for the sound of sucking water. I expect to see a deer pop its head up out of the tall grass. I make noise, talking to the dog, and call out according to our taboo, "Grandfather, Grandmother, I'm just picking cranberries. Thank you. Gunalchéesh. Giitu."

The knoll turns out to be full of mossy fallen logs with waist-high grass surrounding them. The area is dense with highbush cranberry bushes. I make my way toward them, using my body to push through the grass. I climb up on the logs as Kéet effortlessly jumps up behind me. From the top of the log I look back across the road and see my grandchildren and my daughters picking berries. The lake is a deep blue and the sun is warm on my face. I reflect on our values: harmony with nature, to live in balance with nature. I'm surrounded by bushes adorned with highbush cranberries. I fill my bucket.

We meet back at the picnic table for lunch. As we eat, I talk about another Sámi value: shared wealth. Later, back at the fishcamp, we will clean the berries and freeze them in plastic baggies so they'll stay good for up to two years. I'll get to jelly making and experimenting later in the fall and winter. In addition to jelly, ketchup, and fruit leather, I might add the highbush cranberry pulp and juice to muffins and breads. My grandchildren know whatever we make with the cranberries we're going to share or give away. They know they've picked these berries for others.

Our break is over and we make our way through the small trail beside the picnic table into the bushes. We bend branches down to reach the berries, climb atop stumps, and jump over bog puddles. After another half hour we're tired and our hands are cold, our clothing is wet, and we have picked more berries. It's time to go home so we can enjoy the September afternoon sun on our deck, sitting around a table, sipping hot chocolate, and cleaning leaves and stems from our berries.

HIGHBUSH CRANBERRY JELLY

MAKES 10 JARS

Cranberry jelly warms a winter day when you serve it on pilot bread. You can make it with fresh berries in the fall and use this jelly all year round. Gift the jelly with a box of Alaska's cherished pilot bread crackers for the holiday. The process below includes how to make cranberry juice on the stove, but my daughter Nikka recommends using a steam juicer, which is like a giant double boiler with a hose or spout. After you make the juice, then you can add it to your pot with the pectin and begin from there.

5 cups highbush cranberries

3 cups water, plus more as needed

1 (1.75-ounce) package powdered pectin (see note)

4 cups sugar

2 teaspoon lemon juice

Prepare your canning jars first by sterilizing the jars, lids, and rings. Wash everything in hot, soapy water, and then boil the jars for at least 10 minutes and leave them in simmering water until they're ready to use.

Put the berries and water in a 2-quart pot over medium-high heat. As the berries heat up, use a potato masher to gently crush them and release their juices. Bring the berries to a boil and gently boil for 10 minutes, or simmer for about 30 minutes. Keep an eye on the water level, adding a bit more if needed to make sure the berries don't scorch.

Drape cheesecloth over a colander and place the colander in a pot or bowl in the sink. Carefully pour the cooked berries and their juices into the cheesecloth-lined colander, letting the juice drip into the bowl. When the berries have cooled sufficiently, use tongs to squeeze the berries in the cheesecloth, pushing any leftover juice into the bowl. Jelly-making purists don't squeeze the liquid from the berries, but I do. This should yield 5 to 6 cups of juice.

Measure 4½ cups of the highbush cranberry juice (add water if needed to supplement). Pour the juice into a clean 2-quart pot over high heat. Add the pectin and mix it into the juice with a wooden spoon or whisk. Bring the juice and pectin to a boil over high heat, stirring constantly. Add the sugar and lemon juice. Bring the mixture to a full rolling boil without stirring, then turn off the heat and skim off any foam on the top.

Pour the mixture into sterilized jars, until about ¼ inch from the top. Wipe off the jar rims with a clean hot towel. Put on the sterilized lids and rings and place in a large pot. Fill the pot with water so the jars are completely submerged into hot water and boil for about 10 minutes.

Carefully remove the jars with tongs or a jar lifter. Let cool for 12 hours. The jelly can be used when it's completely set, which can sometimes take up to a couple of days. Jars of homemade jelly can be kept for up to a year on a shelf in a cool dark place.

Note: You can substitute 1 (3-ounce) package liquid pectin like Certo. Instructions will differ if you're using liquid pectin because it's typically added at the end of the boiling process. Follow the instructions on the pectin package.

LISTENING TO THE FOREST

"Let's go listen to the forest," I say to my dad. We drive out on our logging roads, taking a couple of berry buckets with us. It's cranberry and Labrador tea season. Kéet is with us. She leans out the truck window, sniffing the chilly air. My dad pulls his truck off to the side of the dirt road. Near a muskeg with easy access, we step out of the truck. Every sound has a sense of newness to him, sounds he hasn't heard in thirty to forty years. My dad was nearly deaf, but now, with the help of his new hearing aids, he can hear.

The first day he wore his new hearing aids, he said, "I can hear my footsteps. I can hear myself breathing." The audiologist had cautioned that returning to the hearing world would not be easy. My dad complains I'm clanking dishes when I cook. He tells me not to yell at him while we're driving to town to do errands. I'd been talking loudly at him for years because he was nearly deaf and now he can hear. But he's not always irritated by what he can now hear again. He can hear bald eagles in the nearby tree screeching every morning and the ducks bathing in the creek next door.

While in flight, bald eagles' specialized auricular feathers funnel sounds directly into their ears.

Beside the muskeg, my dad stands still listening to the sounds he hasn't heard in years, sounds I take for granted: the blue jays squawking, the creek rushing around boulders, another car approaching, the wind. "I missed all the bird sounds," he says. "That's what I missed most. I missed the hooters." I listen too for the sooty grouse, common in Southeast Alaska.

I walk deeper into the muskeg for cranberries and Kéet remains near my dad as he picks the Labrador tea beside the road. A while later, Kéet gives a low growl and looks up the steep hillside to the game trail leading into the thicker woods. My dad stops picking. Kéet growls again and then woofs. My dad raises his voice and says, "Kéet is growling toward the woods."

Dogs hear higher frequencies than humans. What a human can hear at twenty feet away, dogs can detect at eighty feet. A dog's ear muscles, as many as eighteen of them, allow the dog to move its ears in the direction of a sound.

I walk back to the road, watching the surrounding woods. "Good dog, Kéet," I say. We don't wait to see what might bound over the hill or crack through the bushes. The week before, my dad wouldn't have heard the dog's warning, even if he had been standing right next to her.

We hop back into the truck and drive slowly with the windows rolled down, noting the sounds along the way. "Do you hear that?" I ask my dad as we drive by the creek, its sounds swishing in and out of our hearing range. "Did you hear that crack and snap? Do you hear that bird?"

Trees make noise as they grow and interact with their environment. Drought-stressed trees make sounds—their thirsty sound is beyond our hearing capabilities.

We pass a stand of large yellow cedars. A sound moves toward us, coming through the trees like wind. It sounds like a barking dog, but then I realize it's a raven. Ravens are smart and have sharp eyesight and hearing. Is it addressing us? The bird is not at the edge of the forest but flying through the branches, the air moving through old man's beard. In my mind there's an image and a knowing associated with what I'm hearing. Ravens imitate all kinds of sounds including our voices and other animals. The raven caws. "Did you hear that?" I say, turning toward my dad.

He is smiling. "Yes, I did."

Ravens make at least thirty-three different vocalizations that can be gurgles, croaks, raspy calls, shrill calls, knocks, bill snaps, water drops, gratings, kraws, caws, crucks, and tockings.

At the next picking stop, we get out of the truck and Kéet bounds into the muskeg. We follow her while two bald eagles circle overhead. My dad hears the eagles, looks up, and points a finger ahead. He tells me there's something dead over there. "Maybe it's the moose that was illegally shot a week or so ago," he says. "We shouldn't hang out here. There could be something feeding on the carcass."

I call Kéet and we head back to the truck. Our footfalls squish down into the muskeg. We listen for faraway sounds, for growls and cracks and rustles. Our safety and well-being in the forest is dependent upon our hearing. Of course I knew that, but I hadn't thought about how much my dad was disabled by his deafness. Now, though, each season is going to bring new discoveries: the sound of snow, winter gulls, a rain squall, and the morning birds of spring.

Deer have hearing acuity similar to humans, but their ears move independently of each other, picking up on the sounds of potential danger from all directions.

Back home at the fishcamp, we sit outside on the deck. My dad spots a big humpback whale across the water near the Etolin Island shore. We watch, searching the gray sea. Suddenly the whale surfaces again, blows, and glides back in. The sound of the exhale is exciting, even more so for my dad. This is the first time in decades he's heard a whale exhale. After a few minutes, the whale surfaces again right in front of the fishcamp, lets out two song notes, then arches and heads down into the sea. We laugh. *Wow, that was cool.*

Amazing. It's one of those moments you share with another person thinking, *Did that wonderful thing really just happen?*

"That tune was for you," I say to my dad. I really believe it was.

The next day my dad shows me his small notebook with something written in it. He hands it to me. "I wrote a poem," he says. I read it and I'm surprised and delighted. He's an Elder now and he says it's the first time he's written a poem. This hearing journey has inspired him to take the time to stop and enjoy the world around him.

This poem is food for the soul! With my dad's permission
I'm sharing the poem with you, Dear Reader. Enjoy.

STOP THE SHOUTING AND LISTEN TO THE SUNSET
by Mitchell (Mickey) Prescott

I guess I've been missing this most
if not all my life, to hear sounds
I've never heard before.
It's a new world
to hear the rain
to hear the wind
to hear the waves
to hear the birds
to hear people
talking,
to hear them walking,
to hear the fish flopping,
to hear the hooters
hooting.
To hear the dogs
barking, it scares me each
time.
But to think how much I missed
with my children
and grandchildren
and great-grandchildren.
Maybe this is why
I'm still here!
So stop the shouting
and listen to the sunset.

STINK CURRANTS
AND LANDSLIDES

Waterfalls rush down the hillside as my dad and I drive around the bluffs. We pass a truck-sized boulder on the side of the road at 8-Mile beach and I ask, "Isn't this where the slide that almost got you came down?"

My dad looks in his rearview mirror as if to remind himself. "Yeah," he says, "back there a bit. My friend and I were heading out hunting one morning in the fall. We were driving along near here. Up ahead we saw a waterfall suddenly turn muddy. We knew something was going on up there. Twigs and rocks started churning through the water. I asked my friend if we should continue and he said, 'Hit it!' So I floored it and drove through rushing dirty water. I looked in the mirror behind us and there was a gush of brown water, and then a big log burst out and covered the whole highway, both lanes. If we'd been right there, we would've been squished. It was something to see a log shoot right out of that waterfall about twenty feet in the air!"

I'm cautious since we're heading to an old avalanche basin and it's been raining for a while now. "It's landslide weather" is a common local saying in a rainy year, so we've been hesitant to go out to pick stink currants. But it's been dry for a couple of days in a row, so we decided we'd better get out before the ripe currants fall off the bushes.

Stink currants—also known as gray currants, blue currants, or stinking black currants—love our rainforest: the wet bluff areas, stream edges, old landslides, and hillsides. Living in Southeast, both my dad and I have seen the blue-gray berries in the woods. My dad has never picked them before, but I ate them as a kid whenever I happened upon them. Stink currants taste like a combination of a small grape and a currant. They're tart and not too sweet. My dad said he didn't even know they were edible. I learned more about them in Sitka when I harvested with a few locals who said they were a favorite.

My dad and I drive a couple miles out the logging road until we turn and drive up a hill to where the road forks and gets even bumpier and narrower. Bushes scratch the side of the truck.

"There!" I've spotted the place we'd scoped out before. Last year we'd missed the opportunity to pick currants because they'd already dropped off the branches. Now there are lots of them. We park in a pull-off area and grab our buckets from the back of the truck. Kéet sniffs the grass and I can already smell the currants.

How do I describe the scent of stink currants? It's vanilla-like, earthy, with a tinge of medicine. The interesting scent comes from yellow glands dotting the plant. Some would describe it as "skunky." I know people who don't like the smell so they avoid the berries, but I love it. I step down into the ditch where the berries hang around me like small gray-blue grapes. I sniff the leaves and inhale memory: childhood hillsides near my home, playing in creeks, picnics on beaches.

Stink currants grow in Southeast Alaska and down along the Pacific Northwest coast to as far as Northern California. Their Latin name is *Ribes bracteosum* and they're related to other currants and gooseberries. Their leaves are fairly big and look hairy, and they can grow up to nine feet tall. Stink currants have both male and female organs and are pollinated by insects like dragonflies and butterflies. They bloom in May and June and the berries start to ripen in late summer, anywhere from August to September, and you can even find a few stink currants hanging on the bushes in October if the wind hasn't blown them off.

My dad leans on his cane and steps down into the wet ditch. A red plastic Folgers coffee can, serving as a homemade berry bucket, hangs around his neck. He picks berries from the bushes in front of him. "These are easy to pick," he says.

"Shaax̱," I say remembering the Lingít name for the berry. My dad repeats the word.

According to Tlingit Oral Tradition, Raven created shaax̱ by throwing a blanket onto the sea and letting it float to shore where he tossed it on the bushes. The berries grew from his blanket.

Many Northwest Coast Indigenous Peoples—the Tsimshian, Salish, and Tlingit, among others—use stink currants for a variety of things. The berries, leaves, roots, and stems are ingredients for laxative medicines and for treating colds and skin disorders. Their food uses are plenty; stink currants can be in cakes, breads, jams, jellies, pies, and sauces for meat or salmon. But eating large quantities of the fresh berries can cause an upset stomach. This is probably why an old recipe for preserving the berries suggests mixing stink currants with other berries, adding salmon eggs, then adding some hooligan grease and pressing them into round cakes and drying them. Some people make a pudding with oats and the berries. Stink currants can be frozen for use all year long. Sounds good to me!

Now, as I'm encircled in that sweet, odd scent, I look up and consider the bare hillside and the mountain ridge above me. There was once a large avalanche here, with snow, trees, and rocks tumbling down and transforming the landscape. The stink currants sure love this area. Finding a tree root to press my foot against, I grasp a strong branch and heave myself up from the ditch. I'm up above my dad now on a steep embankment and start picking. As we collect berries, we listen for growls, birds squawking their warnings, and rumbles and snaps and rushing water. But we also tell stories. Stories and berry picking go together like a father and daughter filling buckets with stink currants.

"Tell me Grandpa Pressy's landslide story," I say. "The one when he was out fishing."

My dad picks berries and plops them into the bucket as he tells the story.

"He was fishing Back Channel on the *Mercedes*. It was this time of year, sometime in the 1960s. It had been storming and raining. He decided to go to Ham Island, which is really named Blake Island, to fish and he started down the channel. He got halfway there and on the mainland shore he saw there were two or three landslides that had come all way down to the water. It happened before he'd gotten there. Logs were piled up in the channel in from of him and he couldn't get the boat through. It took days before the landslide broke up enough for a passage again. You can see the landslide area today. It slid from about two thousand feet up all the way down to the water. It must've been something to see."

"Wow," I say. "I'll bet there are stink currants growing there now."

My dad considers this. "I'd guess there would be."

After our three buckets are full, our fingers stained purple, and our minds rich with stories, we pile our soggy selves and the wet dog into the truck. With the scent of vanilla and leaves and earth on our clothes and hair, we drive away from the avalanche basin, down the hill, over bumps and rocks, on the lookout for more locations where Raven had tossed his blanket into the bushes. We will be back next season to pick berries and fill the forest again with our stories.

STINK CURRANT JELLY

MAKES 12 JARS

*Whale watching, counting fish jumps, storytelling,
and stink currant jelly go together. Sit outside on
your porch with your favorite Elder and share
stink currant jelly on crackers.*

8 cups stink currants (also called gray currants)	1 (1.75-ounce) package powdered pectin
1 cup water, plus more	7 cups sugar

Prepare your canning jars first by sterilizing the jars, lids, and rings. Wash everything in hot, soapy water, and then boil the jars for at least 10 minutes and leave them in simmering water until they're ready to use.

In a large pot, combine the stink currants and the water. Crush the currants in the pot with a potato masher or the bottom of a cup to release the juices. Simmer over low heat until the berries have broken down and released all their juices, about 15 to 20 minutes. Add water, up to ½ cup, if the mixture looks too dry.

Drape a cheesecloth over a colander and place the colander into a bowl. Pour the simmered berries through the cheesecloth and let the juice drip through into the bowl. Some people like to squeeze the cheesecloth with tongs to help the juice flow through, while others prefer to let gravity do the work. Measure out 6½ cups of the currant juice for this recipe. Freeze the berry pulp or leftover juice in a container for another use.

In a large pot, stir the 6½ cups of the currant juice with the powdered pectin. Place over high heat and stir constantly until you reach a full rolling boil that can't be stirred down—in other words, when you stir, the boil shouldn't recede. Stir in the sugar, then bring to a full rolling boil again. Boil hard for 1 minute, stirring constantly. Take the pot off the heat and skim off the foam.

Pour the stink currant juice into the sterilized jars, leaving about ¼-inch space at the top. Wipe off the jar rims with a clean hot towel before putting the sterilized lids and rings on. Put the jars in a large pot and fill the pot with water until the jars are completely submerged. Then carefully remove the jars with tongs or a jar lifter. Let cool. Jars of homemade jelly can be kept for a up to a year on a shelf in a cool, dark place.

WINTER BLUES

I put a handful of blueberries into a Mason jar filled with water, add a few sprigs of spring-growth Labrador tea, and, for good measure, throw in several spruce tips. I let the water steep for a few minutes. Blueberries are my remedy for the winter blues, and by that I mean they are an energy pick-me-up. Sometimes it's hard to get through the last part of winter, especially when I know spring is right around the corner.

As I sip the blueberry water, I'm transported back to mid-July to the "family blueberry spot," as we call it. I'm standing next to my daughter Nikka and my newborn grandson James, also called Bear, and our family nearby. Nikka's picking blueberries with Bear in a carrier strapped to her chest. This is Bear's first outing into the wilderness and he's only two weeks old.

We call this blueberry patch the family spot because there's parking, a picnic table, and a trail that is easily accessible for Elders. Grandson Jackson and I leave Nikka and Grandson Bear near the trail, and we make our way through the bushes to a large berry patch. Grandson Timothy follows his Great-grandpa Mickey further down the trail.

As I pick, my hands, lips, and tongue turn purple; my grandkids and I are sampling the berries today. At least two varieties of blueberries surround us—I can tell by the size of the bushes and the shape of the leaves. I pull a branch out to show Jackson. "See, this one is shiny and dark. These are black huckleberries. You can pick those into the bucket too."

There are a few blueberry varieties in Alaska: the oval-leaf blueberry, the Alaskan blueberry, the dwarf blueberry, the black huckleberry, and the lowbush blueberry. In different parts of Alaska these varieties are often called other names. The Alaskan blueberry is thought to be a hybrid from the oval-leaf and the red huckleberry. With the exception of the lowbush variety, I don't separate them when picking because they grow in the same areas.

Black huckleberry bushes, Vaccinium membranaceum, *can grow to be over six feet high.*

Surrounded by blueberries, Nikka sits on a stump and nurses her fussy baby. Soon Bear is quiet and she starts picking again. Great-grandpa Mickey coughs in the bushes so we know where he is.

"Where are you?" I yell out to Grandson Timothy.

A large bush wiggles near his great-grandfather. "Over here," Timothy yells.

We pick for about an hour before everyone decides we're done. We have four generations of blueberry-pickers with us. There's nothing like smelling like berries and leaves and moss at the end of the day. This fond memory has carried me through the end of the summer, into fall, and now through the winter.

We share our love of blueberries with the bears, deer, squirrels, moose, grouse, ptarmigans, and thrushes.

I sip the blueberry water and sigh, remembering the smell of the bushes and the warm sun. Soon I'll be watching for the first blueberry blossoms. I'm hoping this last cold spell is the final one of the winter. Bear will be a year old when blueberry season arrives again and that'll bring new challenges as we bring him out to pick berries with us. And we'll have to figure out how not to say his name Bear out loud in the woods.

Although the Alaskan blueberry-picking season is anywhere

Nikka Mork and her infant son, James "Bear" Hurst, pick blueberries.

from the end of June to mid-October depending on the region and weather patterns, winter is also a time for eating berries. Like us, animals depend on the blueberry plants for their winter browsing. Animals browse on the bushes, and we browse on what we've put up in the freezer. The Alaskan blueberry is found in shallower snow beneath older growth, which makes it more accessible to browsers.

This winter, my daughter Nikka is teaching Grandson Bear to love our traditional subsistence foods. So far, he's not too sure about the tart berries. They're good nutrition for the long winter days because they're high in fiber and carbohydrates and a good source of vitamin C, niacin, and manganese. They're a dose of Vitamin Happiness: blueberries help control blood sugar and have a calming effect, and can increase serotonin levels and help those suffering from PTSD, anxiety, and depression. A bowl of blueberries improves winter sluggishness. The antioxidants in the blueberries stimulate oxygen flow to the brain.

The most widespread of all the Alaskan
blueberries is the lowbush blueberry.

My oldest daughter Vivian says blueberries are a "superfood." Superfoods like salmon, blueberries, and seaweed are nutritionally dense and have significant health benefits. As a traditional foods specialist, Vivian helped test the antioxidant levels in some of Alaska's edibles alongside the researchers at the University of Alaska who studied Alaska's blueberries. Antioxidants are micronutrients essential to our body's metabolism. They block oxidation's destructive effects, hence the name antioxidants. Blueberries are also anti-inflammatory and protect against cell damage that can lead to Alzheimer's, cancer, and heart disease.

Oxygen Radical Absorbance Capacity (ORAC) analysis measures a food's antioxidant activity. The wild Alaskan blueberry earns a score of 76 compared to farmed or cultivated blueberries, which test at 30. Lower 48–grown wild blueberries measure at 61, while Alaska's oval-leaf blueberry scores 111, our dwarf blueberry 85, and our bog blueberry scoring 77. That's a big difference!

Interestingly, home processing, such as freezing, and drying does not diminish the blueberry's antioxidant levels. We make some jelly and jam with our blueberries, but mostly we freeze them. In the winter I make blueberry smoothies, tarts and pies, muffins, and pancakes, as well as blueberry butter and blueberry buckle. I drink blueberry iced tea and blueberry lemonade and add blueberries to my cereal and oatmeal.

A single Alaskan blueberry can have more than a hundred seeds.

After decades of harvesting blueberries, the days seem to run together, but then a taste of a tart berry floating in water takes me back into the bushes: watching my grandson's small hands pluck a berry and pop it into his mouth, listening to a grandfather telling stories, and having a picnic of smoked salmon spread on pilot bread followed by homemade cookies. Vitamin Happiness for the winter blues.

BLUEBERRY WATER

MAKES 1 CUP

Years ago, I hiked the Chilkoot Trail sipping blueberry-and-devil's-club-bark-infused waters. Infused waters are popular with Alaskan hikers and outdoor enthusiasts, and Alaska Native health organizations promote drinking infused waters from local ingredients to replace sugary drinks. But, of course, Elders have always talked about the benefits of using natural plants in water. If you want to make iced tea instead of water, add a cold-brew teabag or mix this blueberry water with your favorite brewed tea. Add a few blueberries to your favorite hot tea too.

¼ cup blueberries

1 to 2 sprigs of spring-growth Labrador tea or Labrador tea leaves

3 to 4 frozen or dried spruce tips

Sweetener to taste (optional)

In a Mason jar, combine the blueberries, Labrador tea, and spruce tips. Fill the jar with water and let everything steep for a few minutes before drinking. You can strain, or leave the blueberries, tea leaves, and spruce tips in with your water. Add a healthy sweetener, like honey, if you like.

WINTER BLUEBERRY SMOOTHIE

MAKES 5 TO 6 CUPS

Blueberries are Vitamin Happiness! I make smoothies all year round, but there's nothing like drinking smoothies during the long Alaskan winters. My grandchildren love smoothies, and I can sneak in all kinds of good-for-you berries or plants, even spruce tips. This blueberry smoothie is so versatile as you can use any combination of fruit (or even vegetables, like shredded carrot or kale) you have on hand.

½ to 1 cup chopped fruit, such as apples, strawberries, oranges, bananas, or kiwis

½ to 1 cup blueberries

¼ cup spruce tips

1 cup fruit juice, such as orange or cranberry juice

3 to 4 heaping tablespoons plain Greek yogurt

Honey or sweetener to taste

Ice

Coconut or almond milk

In a blender, combine the chopped fruit, blueberries, spruce tips, fruit juice, Greek yogurt, and honey. Add a handful of ice. Fill the rest of the blender with the milk, leaving some room at the top to allow the blender to blend. Start by using the chop setting to begin blending the ingredients, then blend on high for a minute to make sure everything is well mixed. Pour into glasses and serve cold.

SALMON HEAD SOUP

Heat up a couple quarts of water in large pot, add an onion and a salmon head, and boil the mixture until it turns white. In my family, we drink this for medicine. This is Hoonah Elder Mamie Williams's recipe for salmon head broth, commonly used in Tlingit culture to combat and prevent the flu. Many Hoonah residents also use this recipe to ease their flu symptoms.

Nutritionally, not all salmon are the same; wild salmon have significantly more vitamin D than farmed salmon, and salmon varieties have different nutritional values. Salmon head soup is a good food during the cold and flu season because salmon is high in vitamins A, C, D, and E as well as omega-3 fatty acids.

Despite colonization, salmon head soup has continued to be a staple in Alaskan Native diets. Fish head soup is part of my children's identity. My daughter Vivian says, "Salmon chowder is one of my Grandpa Elmer's favorite foods." Their T'akdeintaan Clan story tells of a kittiwake (sea pigeon) that saved them. Vivian tells the story:

"I've heard different versions of the story, so forgive me if I get it wrong. One year, winter lasted long and spring didn't come soon enough, so people were hungry. People were going to starve. A young girl had a pet kittiwake and decided to set it free. Instead of just leaving, though, the kittiwake brought back fish for the girl and she made soup with it. The bird did this every day until spring came and it saved everyone from starvation. That's why I am here today—because of that generous little bird and fish soup."

In Southeast Alaskan communities, salmon head soup is an important part of our gift economy. In addition to Alaska Native families, many people with Scandinavian or Filipino heritage enjoy this food tradition. Wrangell residents Vincent and Lynn Balansag have told me, "Fish head soup is a comfort food for us Filipinos. It is a casual food we enjoy with family and friends, around the table, in shorts and tank tops, with one foot on a chair. It's usually made and eaten the day after a fiesta, the light and refreshing taste washing away hangovers and leveling out the heavy food eaten the day before."

In Southeast Alaska, we brew our fish broth medicines and share them with friends and family. Fishermen gift fish heads to Elders or others who can't get out to the water easily. We gift fish heads to people we know who are susceptible to illness during the flu season, as well as to family and friends. A gift of salmon heads shows you you're loved.

"My Grandpa Frank Young was Haida, a fisherman and local Wrangell barber," says Twyla Ingle Olson, who was born and raised in Wrangell. "He always had a pot of salmon heads boiling on the stove. When I was five, I traded my grandpa all of my Halloween candy for a garbage bag full of salmon heads. He later gave the candy back to my mother."

In a salmon-head gifting economy, fishermen give Elders salmon heads, and in turn Elders teach the younger generation the art of making broth, soups, and chowders from the fish heads. Fellow Wrangellite Laura Gile says, "My gramma Sarah Pearl (Paratrovich) Wigg used to make fish head soup. I remember there was seaweed and salmon eggs in it, and she would eat it over rice with the broth poured on the top. I also remember her saying that the eyes were a delicacy."

Some people simmer fish broth for four to five hours and use it in noodle soup or other recipes. Some save it to drink as medicine later. Preparing salmon head soup can be problematic for some. Vivian once tried to make salmon head soup at a non-Native friend's house. Vivian says, "She got upset because she thought it stunk up her house. She was also disgusted by the fish heads I saved in the freezer."

Wrangellite Heidi Armstrong told me her dad was the one who made fish head soup in her family. "He'd brown onions and celery and add water and fish heads. The heads would boil till cooked, and then just before serving, he'd add a can or two of canned milk. He'd serve it with black seaweed. We could add salt and pepper as needed. Also, we'd bake fish heads as well, cutting the fish head in half and baking it. Oh, yum!"

As I sip the salmon head broth I've made, I'm reminded not everyone can stomach eating fish eyeballs or smelling fish soup simmering on the stove. As a kid, Vivian was grossed out when people popped the fish eyeballs in their mouths. Vivian doesn't mind eating them now, but they aren't her favorite part. "My favorite parts are the salmon cheeks," she says.

Many of my Native and Filipino friends eat the whole salmon head. When it comes to eating a fish head, the Balansags tell me, "Filipinos utilize almost every part of the animal when it comes to cooking. We don't like throwing away a part of something we bought if we can still make something out of it. Growing up in the Philippines where money is hard to come by, it goes against the grain for Filipinos to waste food." The Balansags also explain, "Fish head soup usually goes together with fried fish. The whole fish is cleaned, with the head cut lengthwise and set aside for fish head soup, and the body cut and salted for frying. This way, we utilize almost all of the fish and minimize waste."

Mya DeLong, a local Wrangell florist and fisherman on the F/V *Trendsetter*, says, "I made my first batch of fish head soup last summer with fresh herbs I grew. My garden was heavily producing herbs at the time. I separated the pieces around the collar and made sure to eat the eyeballs too. I made a ramen with the broth. Delicious!"

Vivian was gifted salmon heads from two of her fisherman friends: "From these two heads we'll make both broth and soup. Two heads can make a lot of broth, so we'll freeze half of the broth for use later. We'll split the other half to make soup recipes and give part of the broth away. When making soup, we try to use accompanying ingredients filled with lots of nutrients known to fight colds and the flu. First, we make a ginger fish head soup using coconut cream, ginger, garlic, shallots, spinach, kale, and mushrooms.

Then we make another soup with garlic, onions, potatoes, carrots, mushrooms, green onions, and lots of bacon. I season them both with salt and pepper."

What concerns me most about making salmon head soup, both for medicine and well-being, is the increasing lack of salmon. Climate change and overfishing has something to do with smaller harvests and smaller fish. Lack of access to our subsistence salmon is affecting how we are conveying knowledge to the next generation. The acts of gifting salmon and teaching through story and recipes are important parts of our traditional education. Indigenous knowledge is embedded in our Clan story about the girl who saved a village with fish soup; it instructs us to eat fish head soup to boost our immune systems.

Let's not lose this knowledge. Let's keep our fish head soup stories and memories going. We are connected to everything here, even salmon heads, so we need a healthy ecosystem; this includes the herring that salmon eat, and the ocean and rivers salmon live in. Let's stay healthy and share with others. Salmon head soup is good medicine. Eat your salmon head soup and don't forget to eat the eyeballs.

SALMON HEAD SOUP

MAKES ABOUT 6 SERVINGS

In Alaska we don't like to waste food since we work so hard at providing subsistence foods for our families. Even our Indigenous stories warn us about wasting food. This recipe is courtesy of fellow Wrangellites Vincent Balansag and Lynn Torres Balansag, acquaintances of mine. Vince, Lynn, and their children are immigrants who've settled in Wrangell, continuing our Alaskan island's tradition of welcoming families from the Philippines.

1 plum (Roma) tomato, quartered
½ red onion, sliced
¼ red bell pepper
1 stalk lemongrass, folded in fourths and bundled with kitchen string
3 cups water
1 salmon head, cut in half lengthwise

Salt or Lawry's Seasoning Salt to taste
Chopped green onions
Handfuls of baby spinach or baby bok choy
Hot cooked rice, for serving

In a large pot, combine the tomato, red onion, red bell pepper, lemongrass, and water. Bring to a boil over high heat and let boil for about 5 minutes. Add the salmon head pieces and season with salt, then continue boiling for another 5 minutes to build a flavorful broth. Add the green onions and baby spinach or bok choy right away and remove from the heat. Leave the salmon head in the soup, but remove the inedible lemongrass bundle. Serve immediately over piping-hot rice.

THE PRACTICE OF GIFTING

I fold two heaping tablespoons of chopped spruce tips into the cookie batter. I'm making spruce tip holiday sugar cookies to gift to family. Spruce tips are my favorite treats from nature, so it makes sense to gift something that's been gifted to me. In my Sámi way of knowing, láhi is a gift worldview, meaning the land provides gifts. Láhi is a *relationship* between humans and the land, a way of life. It's similar to "Haa atxaayí haa ḵusteeyíx̱ sitee," meaning "Our food is our way of life" in the Tlingit culture.

My dad bags smoked hooligan and smoked salmon to share. He carves beads, walking sticks, fishing gear, and deer calls fashioned out of wood, all with the intention of gifting. The practice of gifting is not only about holidays—it's a way of walking the world, no matter your spiritual practices. We feel the spirit this time of year: Hanukkah, Kwanzaa, Yule, Las Posadas, Simbang Gabi, and more. Our practices and beliefs include giving rituals as some of the ways we maintain relationships. In other words, we give because it's who we are.

Grandson Jonah helps pack five cases of jams and jellies to deliver to our local Tribal office. Gifting is all around him. He's been learning to gift since he was a baby. It's a part of his Tlingit, Alutiiq, and Potawatomi heritage too. Unfortunately, colonization and its inherent paternalism tried to eradicate gift economies around the

Harvesting spruce tips. The red cedar basket was woven by Wrangellite Faye Khort.

world by outlawing gifting ceremonies, and redefining "family" to guide subsistence and bartering laws. Many of the laws go against a deeply held Sámi value that society is based upon cultural pluralism and the extended family—our roots are remembered. Family is not just defined as a "household" or people related by blood. Modern regulations often ignore complex relationships, as if Indigenous Peoples cannot govern their own economies.

The Sámi value that material wealth is shared and given away is inherent in understanding láhi, our gifts from the land. We catch halibut, package the fillets, and share them with family. Crab is cleaned and cooked and gifted. We pack up jarred smoked salmon for daughters and sons and grandchildren. My Grandpa Al, my mother's dad, gifted me a case of smoked salmon every Christmas when I was a young adult. He's gone now, but every time I see an old-style tin of salmon, I think of him.

The practice of gifting is part of many Indigenous origin stories. The first plant, fish, or animal is often said to have been given to humans as a gift to be taken care of, nurtured, and respected, and a relationship develops. Sámi received wild reindeer as a gift from the

Sun's daughter. Gifting asserts our identity and our relationships, that we're still here and still sharing and thriving. Even with the rules and regulations for fishing and harvesting, the practice of gifting is a decolonizing act. During the COVID-19 pandemic, gifting has been difficult. Still, we beaded, we wrote, we carved and wove, and we produced plays. We worked. We took care of others. We offered something. We gifted jam and jelly and fresh berries and shared halibut.

So how do you teach gifting? An important Sámi value is that our teachings come from nature and family Elders. Our gifting is collective and a part of our community. It's called attáldat, a Sámi term meaning our community as a whole, not the individual. Attáldat is giving and sharing in order to sustain the community. Children watch what we do. Grandsons Timothy, Jackson, and Jonah have helped bag up spruce tips for gifting. Grandson Bear, just a year old, is learning how to gift. They're watching our gifting practices during this pandemic. Did we take care of our Elders, our families and friends, and strangers? What gifts did we offer up? How we respond could reverberate for generations. This doesn't mean we hide our struggles; it means we're honest with our younger generation about what we're going through and how they can help us through these times. We might not be able to visit our grandparents, but maybe a young person can help us come up with creative solutions. My grandsons get on Zoom and play games with their great-grandpa.

Much has been written about the gift economy, the gift worldview, and the gift culture. In Southeast Alaska we're familiar with the ku.éex', meaning "the pay-off party," the Tlingit memorial ceremony, and other potlatch or reciprocal traditions. In our multicultural family, teaching gifting is important: it's what we do at our fishcamp. We pay our respects. Sámi pay respect by leaving gifts or offerings at sacred sites. Some might be surprised to know that thousands of miles from Sápmi, those of us who are a part of the Sámi diaspora in North America still practice our traditions. We gift to the land.

In these hard times, our Southeast Alaskan gifting culture has been even more apparent. A Wrangellite launched a burial assistance program, another formed a quarantine support group, and someone else created a local Facebook food-share page. The Wrangell Mariners' Memorial, currently under construction, is a gift to our community, a place to honor our fishermen. A local LGBTQIA group, Community Roots, gifted books on diversity of people to teens and younger children. Our local Tribal agency, Wrangell Cooperative Association, in partnership with Sealaska, Orca Bay, and the Alaska Longline Fisherman's Association, gifted coho and rockfish to those in need. We gift in the ways we can even when we don't have much. In the winter, my dad snowplows neighbors' driveways and our walking path and sidewalks with his four-wheeler. It's his gift to the community. Often our gifting goes unnoticed. We don't know who gifted sheetrock to the victims of a trailer fire, or who sent supplies to the town of Haines after a devastating landslide.

This year we've turned to family and friends, our Clans, and our social networks to help get us through the pandemic. Sheltering in place for months is hard. Just when I needed it, a gift came in the mail from my friend Flora Johnson: a pair of exquisitely beaded moccasins. Flora and I have never met in person, but we took online classes together in college and we've corresponded back and forth via Facebook since its launch. Together we brainstormed ideas for her PhD research and have offered advice and encouragement to each other. When I opened the box and saw the moccasins, I cried. I put them on and felt as though I could dance through the pandemic all the way into next year.

I chop spruce tips and fold them into the spruce tip frosting for the cookies. Láhi: the land provided the spruce tips. Gift giving is a way of life and nature is our best teacher. We look to the bunchberries, the gray currants, and the old mossy log rotting in the forest with seedlings sprouting from its bark. We look to the muskegs and streams, and the strait out in front of town. Attáldat is the community. It's a gifting life that sustains us. As we harvest, as we bake, as we open our freezer for berries or fish we've put up, as we load plates of goodies or package up a pair of beaded moccasins to send to a friend, we participate in our biological need to connect, to form relationships, to gift. The practice of gifting is alive and well in Southeast Alaska.

SPRUCE TIP SUGAR COOKIES

MAKES 4 DOZEN COOKIES

Gifts of food to our neighbors, family, and friends says they're loved and appreciated. Gifts made from something you've harvested yourself is extra special.

1 cup (2 sticks) unsalted butter, softened

1½ cups powdered sugar

1 egg

1 teaspoon vanilla or almond extract

½ teaspoon Spruce Tip Juice (page 20)

2 tablespoons finely chopped spruce tips, or more for a stronger flavor

2½ cups all-purpose flour, plus more for rolling

1 teaspoon baking soda

1 teaspoon cream of tartar

SPRUCE TIP FROSTING:

3 cups powdered sugar

¼ tablespoon Spruce Tip Juice (page 20)

4 tablespoons milk

1 tablespoon finely chopped spruce tips (optional)

Spruce tip sugar, for sprinkling (optional)

In a large bowl, combine the butter, powdered sugar, egg, vanilla, and Spruce Tip Juice. Beat with an electric mixer until well blended. Mix in the spruce tips until evenly distributed. Add the flour, baking soda, and cream of tartar and mix until incorporated. Transfer the dough to a lightly floured surface and divide the dough in half. Form the dough into 2 flat disks and cover with plastic wrap. Refrigerate for at least 2 hours.

Preheat the oven to 375°F. On a lightly floured work surface, roll out each dough disk until ¼-inch thick. Use a round or shaped cookie cutter to punch out cookies and place on an ungreased cookie sheet, spaced a couple inches apart. Bake until the edges start to brown, about 7 minutes. Remove from the oven and let the cookies stand for a minute or two on the cookie sheet before cooling completely on a wire rack.

To make the Spruce Tip Frosting, in a large bowl, whisk together the powdered sugar and Spruce Tip Juice. Whisk in the milk 1 tablespoon at a time until the frosting is the right consistency.

When the cookies are completely cool, spread a thick layer of frosting over the top of each cookie. For more spruce tip flavor, sprinkle finely chopped spruce tips or spruce tip sugar over the top.

WINTER KINGS

My dad works the pole and fights the winter king salmon toward the boat where my husband nets the fish and heaves it over the gunwale. It's a cloudy winter day and we've been out for a couple hours now, trolling back and forth in front of the island. The fish is bonked, unhooked, and put into the fish cooler. We bait up, and then my dad resumes his captain's seat at the wheel, ready for the next pass.

Salmon have always been a part of our lives, with the sixth generation of salmon fishermen coming up. My grandson Jonah loves to go fishing, but we weren't able to take him out due to COVID-19. My children's and grandchildren's ancestors have been fishing for salmon in this area for thousands of years, and salmon also school up in our family's Sámi, Finnish, and Irish mythologies. Time is like an endless sea as we troll along slowly. I ask my dad to tell me a story about fishing for winter kings, and he obliges.

"It was a tough winter, probably the early 1960s. My father, your Grandpa Pressy, was out winter fishing in his usual spots and he started catching kings. When the winter winds came up, the boat would ice over and list, so he only fished two hours in the morning. He knew king salmon inside and out and said this day was the largest school of kings he'd ever seen.

"Three of the kings were tagged ones, so he sent the tags in to the

Fish & Game, and it turned out they were from Snake River, Idaho. He loaded the boat down heavy with fish and ended up with a couple boatloads of king salmon."

"What were Idaho salmon doing in Wrangell in the winter?" I ask.

My dad explains the salmon were after the herring that overwinter here. "Herring have certain spots they go to winter. There were a bunch that winter in different areas around Wrangell Island. The big tides in March are when the herring start to spawn nearby."

I was thirteen years old when my grandpa died from a stroke. I imagine Grandpa Pressy as I knew him. In my mind I see his boat, the *Mercedes*, iced over and listing.

Our boat rocks and my husband yells, "Mickey, you've got a fish!" My dad heads out of the cabin onto the back deck. I scoot over to the captain's chair and steer. My dad reels in the fish, but it gets loose, spitting the hook. The poles are rebaited and go back into the water again. My dad takes the wheel again and we continue trolling. Another story flows out into the warm cabin, circling around father and daughter, and I know someday, a grandchild will hear this story too.

"The Alaska Department of Fish and Game once came to my father in the 1950s and asked him if they could hire him and charter his boat for a survey of winter king salmon. He could keep half of the salmon they would catch and measure, and the other half they'd tag and release. He agreed, so they put a holding tank on the boat's back deck and they went to Bradfield Canal. They fished for three days and got eighty kings a day, so he got to keep forty kings for himself each day."

I love salmon stories. I want to learn how to fillet a salmon. I want to know why a winter king tastes so good and why a bright silver salmon makes me think of my Grandpa Pressy. I know him more now than I did when he was alive. My dad will turn another year older in a few months. I feel like time resembles a salmon cycle—it goes on and on and on.

I ask my dad what's different about fishing for winter king salmon. Is there anything I should know?

MY DAD'S TIPS FOR WINTER KING FISHING:

1. The herring that the winter kings eat are scattered around in the winter, so you have to be patient to find them.

2. Fish according to the weather. When it's clear and cold, the wind will come with the sunrise. It's harder to stay on your gear when it's stormy.

3. King salmon are not feeding as much.

4. Winter kings are skittish.

5. When a winter king bites, it's fast and furious. Be ready.

6. Switch your commercial gear to wire leaders. Grandpa Pressy said the monofilaments in commercial gear leave bubbles in the water and the winter kings don't like that. Wire is stealthier. For summer king fishing, though, it doesn't matter.

7. In commercial fishing for winter kings, don't use as many flashers because it scares the salmon. Use plugs—artificial lures made from plastic or wood that look like herring—and spoons because they will outfish flashers two to one. A plug outfishes any bait or other gear.

8. Expect to get more white kings in the winter.

9. For sport fishing, use herring pegs and a two-hook rig to hold the shape of the herring. Winter kings like that.

10. The salmon are also deeper, feeding on the krill.

My dad turns the boat slowly around when we reach the bluffs. He trolls along the bluffs out toward the deeper water, making a bigger circle this time. He tells another story about his experience with winter kings.

"My father once told me about there being a time in February when the winter kings come through, but they are spawners. King salmon live in the ocean for about three to seven years before they come home to spawn. But winter is not usually a time to spawn. He said they showed up like clockwork every winter in this area and he didn't know where they were heading. I thought it was a baloney story. One year, I was fishing by myself on the *Irish* in February, and I happened to be near that area. I had been only catching an occasional winter king. I remembered my father said when the winter kings came, it was like flipping a switch. So I went over there, and I put the gear out, and *bam! Bam!* Nice big spawners, about twenty-five pounds on average. You can tell by the colors and shapes where the kings come from, and these weren't Bradfield or Stikine River or Aaron's Crick kings. I was fishing four poles and the fish were wild, crossing over and tying up the lines. I loaded the boat with fish in a couple days and unloaded those in town and went back and loaded up again."

Now, I consider maybe we should head down to that area my grandfather and my dad fished and see if those salmon do return there "like clockwork," but it's already late in the day and going to get dark soon.

I imagine all those winter kings in our fish hold. I imagine fish scales and slime and blood and all those good images imprinting on the family members of fishermen. I have no idea where those winter kings were going, and my dad doesn't either. Some mysteries should be solved, so my dad and I start planning for next year, to be there at the right moment. But then again, this is the right moment too— trolling for winter kings in front of town, talking salmon stories with my dad.

WHITE KING SALMON CHOWDER

MAKES 8 SERVINGS

In Alaska, we aim to use all parts of the salmon, and making fish broth is a delicious way to do that. You can add any vegetables you like to this chowder, but I like throwing in a handful of chopped spinach and chopped red bell pepper at the end.

Skin, head, and/or bones of 1 salmon

8 cups water

½ cup chopped yellow onion

4 to 6 mushrooms, chopped

2 to 3 stalks celery, chopped

2 tablespoons butter

6 slices smoked bacon, chopped

4 large Yukon Gold, russet, or red potatoes, chopped

¼ cup chopped goose tongue or beach asparagus

¼ cup chopped fresh cilantro

1 teaspoon seaweed seasoning or fresh or dried seaweed

¼ teaspoon freshly ground black pepper

¼ teaspoon garlic powder

2 cups milk (coconut, coconut–almond milk blend, or half-and-half)

1 can corn, regular or creamed

2 cups fresh cooked, flaked white king salmon or 2 (8-ounce) cans white king salmon

Handful of chopped spinach (optional)

Chopped red bell pepper (optional)

To make a broth, place the salmon skin, head, and bones in a large pot with the water. Bring the water to a boil over high heat, then reduce the heat and simmer until the salmon head and pieces are soft, about 30 minutes. Drain the broth through a colander or cheesecloth set over a bowl. Pick out any solids from the broth and set aside.

In a small frying pan, sauté the onions, mushrooms, and celery with the butter until soft and light brown, about 3 minutes. In another pan, cook the bacon until crisp, about 5 minutes.

Transfer the sautéed vegetables and bacon to a large pot. Add 4 cups of the salmon broth (reserve the rest for another use), the potatoes, goose tongue, cilantro, seaweed seasoning, black pepper, and garlic powder. Simmer until the potatoes are almost but not quite done, about 20 minutes. Add the milk, corn, and cooked salmon. Stir in the spinach and red bell pepper, if using, and heat through.

Ladle the chowder into serving bowls and serve hot.

WHAT I'VE LEARNED FROM LIVING AT FISHCAMP

KEEP UP TRADITIONS

Living at fishcamp I've learned it's important to keep up our island traditions. My sister, the longtime host of our family winter game nights, has moved away, but my daughter bought my sister's house, so she inherited game night. There's a new generation taking charge of our nights of food, laughter, and stories. Keeping up our traditions means incorporating our Indigenous values into everything we do. For my adult children, harvesting spruce tips and picking blueberries and fishing for salmon and halibut is about teaching respect and about educating their own children about the medicinal and nutritional value of plants, fish, and deer. Harvesting teaches the ways and values of our Indigenous ancestors.

BE A STUDENT OF LIFE

Fishcamp is a way of life, but the challenge is to make this life sustainable, to preserve the food and to pass on the knowledge of the landscape and traditional foods to family. I'm a student of life, along with my family members. I'm a student of spruce tips and blueberries, and a student of smelt. I'm a student of popweed and devil's club. There are always new things to learn.

My grandchildren sometimes say, "This is the best day of my life," when we're doing something fun together. That's how I feel about the days our family sits alongside the narrow dirt roads, scraping devil's club thorns from its long stalks. I can still smell devil's club juice on my hands.

BE FLEXIBLE

At fishcamp you have to be ready to run out in the boat and set the net when the weather turns good. Be ready to grab the bait, make sandwiches, grab a snack, and get some water. And you have to be flexible, willing to try a fish you've never eaten before. By learning to catch and eat a new fish species, you also learn about its behavior and growth patterns and how to identify it. I have learned to hold a skein of brined dog salmon eggs and gently rub it over a grate, manipulating the bright orange eggs into a bowl. I have learned rainbow smelt have sharp teeth protruding from their tongues, and a superpower called macromolecular antifreeze, allowing them to overwinter beneath ice.

DISCOVER ART

Fishcamp is a place to make art: nature inspires. Thinking like artists, my dad and I travel the logging roads on adventures, searching for new ideas. "Art is everywhere in the forest," my dad once said to me. Over the past couple of years, he's painted an old canoe paddle, designed jewelry from fishing gear, made walking sticks and custom fishing gear, and created art from burls. He even wrote poetry. I make art from old things I find on the beach, and I write. My art rituals cannot be separated from a moment spent resting in a patch of newly emerged skunk cabbage or filling a berry bucket with thimbleberries.

BALANCE AN ISLAND

Balance is one of the most important concepts in the Tlingit culture, as well as in Sámi and Finnish cultures. Though we've learned how to deal with imbalances in nature, we strive to live in balance. Harvesting sea lettuce in the intertidal zone in our sheltered bays teaches us to take enough for ourselves and leave the rest for nature to thrive. We're seeing observable climate changes, so we've had to harvest accordingly, choosing the best times to gather and how much to gather. Too much wind and rain can batter the delicate seaweed.

Too much sun makes it rot. Too much in our basket can leave others behind us hungry. Harvesting sea lettuce teaches us island folk about balance.

SHARE OUR ISLAND FOOD

In Wrangell we live and thrive in a gift economy. Those of us who aren't Tlingit are guests in this land, and we've learned from Tlingit traditions the importance of sharing our knowledge and sharing food. Even though our berry patches and fishing holes are well-kept secrets, we share the bounty we harvest. We learn from the animals and plants who share their lives with us. We maintain interdependent relationships. Like many birds and animals, we love berries. We take only what we need and share with humans and animals alike.

FOSTER COMMUNITY

Everything we do and eat has a sense of community. Labrador tea is the story of us, of the grandkids and Mummo (me) and Great-grandpa, of our community. We are part tea, but also part smoked fish, part grease, part milt, fish eggs, and river sand. We live in an intertwining web of life.

Island folks band together for community runs and walks. We coach and referee school sport teams, we start a chess club, we advocate for LGBTQIA islanders. We eat community moose meat dinners together and help with the senior center because their funding has been cut. We fix up the shooting range and plow snow from the bike path. We stand together to protest mining the Stikine River. We give money to our local radio station and donate a kitchen table to a new couple in town just starting out. We buy a burger at J&Ws for a fundraiser to support a newborn with a disability, and we gather at the Fourth of July Queen's booth to eat deep-fried halibut and coleslaw. We decorate holiday trees to support the local hospice and we hold benefit golfing tournaments in the rainforest among stealthy ravens. These things we do *together* to form an island, Ḵaachxaana.áak'w. Our island lives are thirty miles long and fourteen miles at the widest, and in the shape of a snow goose with wings outstretched, flying to the Stikine River Delta.

Grandson Jackson walks down a muskeg path telling stories
with Great-grandpa Mickey Prescott.

SMELL LIKE FISH AND FOREST

At the end of my life, I want to have lived experiences. I want to pack
memories for my winter months. Scientists say *scent* is the best
trigger of memory: I'm imprinting the scent of tart spruce tips and
pungent skunk cabbage to take me through my elder years. I don't
like washing out the smokehouse-fire scent from my hair. I love my
hoodie with its fishy scent and my gloves wet with rain scent. After
my woven cedar berry bucket gets wet, it smells so good. Our dirt
roads have a scent too, and even the huckleberry leaf in my hair,
and the blue mussel in my pocket carry scentful memories. There's a
perfume of forest and sea, and a palpable and messy sense to my life
at fishcamp. I find myself capturing beach bugs hopping on my floor
and sweeping beach sand out of my sheets. I bring home driftwood
shaped like seahorses and whales, and stones painted by lichen and
geological time to resemble Northwest Coast designs. Every year
I live at the fishcamp, I relearn my messy life. Sometimes I ask
myself, "How did I not know this?" It's okay to make mistakes, to try
something different, to experiment, to fall and get up again. This is
how we learn. And in the process of making a fishcamp life it's okay
to smell like alder fire, to be untidy, and to be so tired you forgot to
pick salmon scales off your face before you go to bed.

MICKEY'S FISHCAMP TIPS

- Always consult with a knowledgeable harvester before you harvest—that doesn't mean checking Facebook or YouTube. Go with a local knowledgeable harvester!

- Don't eat what you don't know.

- Always share your food: people who can't get out to harvest themselves, Elders, low-income families. Share with your local Tribal agency, senior citizen meal center, or veterans center.

- If you're going out harvesting or fishing, go with someone—do not go alone. It can be dangerous work.

- Wear a life jacket when out on the water and be aware of your surroundings on the sea and in the forest.

- Prepare for the wilderness, even if you live in it: tell someone where you are going and when you'll be back, wear appropriate clothing, and bring a cell phone or handheld radio, water, matches or lighter, and some snacks. What you take with you will depend on where you're going and how long you'll be gone.

- Keep a "go-bag" ready with your basic harvesting or fishing supplies in case of emergencies, like "The goose tongue is ripe!" or "I found a salmonberry!"

- Keep a food or subsistence journal: where, when, what, how. Where did you catch that fish? When in the day? What was the weather like? How was the tide? Were you in your skiff or the big boat? Who was with you and what hoochie or bait did you use? My dad writes in his tide book to keep a record and it comes in handy for reference.

- Learn the language of the land: Indigenous language names for things and places. Learn traditional values and ways of knowing connected to where you live and harvest.

- Always be grateful for the gift of nature and the foods and experiences she gifts you and your family.

- Share your wisdom and your recipes.

- If you think you've overcooked your salmon or halibut, let it cool down, flake it up, add whatever from your fridge, and fry it up to make fish patties. Or seafood enchiladas.

- If you're not sure if you should add spruce tips to a recipe, do it anyway.

REFERENCES

For seaweed identification, I used Dr. Dolly Garza's wisdom in *Common Edible Seaweeds in the Gulf of Alaska*. http://alaskacollection. library.uaf.edu/monos/Common%20Edible%20Seaweeds%20in%20 the%20Gulf%20of%20Alaska.pdf

"The Underside of Leaves" This essay first appeared in *Alaska Women Speak*. The italicized lines are quoted from the Salmonberry entry on the USDA Plant Guide and from the following news articles on the Orlando shooting:

Almaguer, Miguel, Gabe Gutierrez, Janet Shamlian, Jon Shuppe. "Diary of a Massacre: How the Orlando nightclub shooting unfolded." *NBC News*. June 13, 2016. https://www.nbcnews. com/storyline/orlando-nightclub-massacre/diary-massacre-how-orlando-nightclub-shooting-unfolded-n590751

Ellis, Ralph, Ashley Fantz, Faith Karimi and Eliott C. McLaughlin. "Orlando shooting: 49 killed, shooter pledged ISIS allegiance." *CNN*. June 13, 2016. https://edition.cnn.com/2016/06/12/us/ orlando-nightclub-shooting/index.html

Flores, Adolfo. "New Details of Pulse Nightclub Shooting are Released: 'If You're Alive, Raise Your Hand.'" *BuzzFeed News*. April 14, 2017. https://www.buzzfeednews.com/article/ adolfoflores/new-details-of-pulse-club-shooting-are-released

"Orlando nightclub shooting." Wikipedia. Accessed September 16, 2021. https://en.wikipedia.org/wiki/ Orlando_nightclub_shooting

"Orlando shooting: Vigils held around the world in wake of mass killing." *ABC NEWS*. June 13, 2016. https://www.abc.net.au/ news/2016-06-14/orlando-shooting-vigils-held-around-the-world/7507260

Reilly, Katie. "Pulse Owner Calls Orlando Nightclub Where Shooter Killed 50 a "Place of Love and Acceptance.'" *Time Magazine*. June 12, 2016. https://time.com/4365603/ orlando-shooting-pulse-nightclub-statement/

Yuhas, Alan with Richard Luscombe. "'Everyone get out and keep running': how the Orlando attack unfolded." *The Guardian*. June 12, 2016. https://www.theguardian.com/us-news/2016/ jun/12/orlando-nightclub-shooting-how-attack-unfolded

"**Skunk Cabbage: A Harbinger of Spring**" The italicized lines are paraphrased from a speech by Willie Marks, Keet Yaanaayí with translation help by Ethel Makinen, Daasdiyáa, and Irene Paul, Yaaxl. aat. Richard Dauenhauer and Nora Marks Dauenhauer, eds., *Haa Tuwunáagu Yís: For Healing Our Spirit*, Tlingit Oratory (Juneau, AK: Sealaska Heritage Institute, 1990).

LINGÍT PRONUNCIATION GUIDE

LINGÍT CONSONANT	LINGÍT WORD	ENGLISH DEFINITION	ENGLISH EXAMPLE (sounds like)
.	wa.e/ naa.át	you/clothes	pause/stop in sound
ch	cheech	porpoise	**ch** as in **ch**ew
ch'	ch'áak'	bald eagle	exaggerated **ch** sound: **ch**alk
d	dáa	weasel	**d**ad
dl	dleit	snow/white	ad**dle**
dz	dzánti	flounder	a**dz**
g	gaaw	drum/time/bell/clock	**g**et
g	gooch	wolf	down in the throat: **g**-uh
gw	a gwéinlí	hoof	**Gw**en
gw	jigwéina	hand towel	use throat: **Gw**en
h	héen	water	**h**ello
j	jánwu	mountain goat	**j**ump
k	kakéin	yarn	**k**it
k'	k'ínk'	fermented fish heads	sharper **k** sound: **k**it
ḵ'	ḵ'eiḵ'w	sea pigeon	down in the throat and pinched quickly: **k**it
kw	kwaan	smallpox	aw**kw**ard
k'w	k'wát'	egg	pinched **kw** sound: aw**kw**ard
ḵw	naaḵw	devil fish/octopus	knoc**kw**
ḵ'w	ḵ'wátl	pot	**c**ut (K-WHATl)
l	lóol	fireweed	**L**-ths
l'	l'ook	coho/silver salmon	airy click with the tongue
n	náayadi	partially dried salmon	**n**ap
s	séew	rain	**s**un
s'	s'eek	black bear	very short **s** sound
sh	shaa	mountain	**sh**ush
t	toowú	mind	**t**ag
t'	t'á	king salmon	sharp **t**
tl	tléik'	no	bot**tle**
tl'	tl'eex	garbage	sharp **tl** sound: bot**tle**
ts	tsaa	seal	**ts**aw
ts'	ts'ats'ée	small songbird	pla-**TES**

LINGÍT CONSONANT	LINGÍT WORD	ENGLISH DEFINITION	ENGLISH EXAMPLE (sounds like)
w	wasóos	cow	**w**ow
x	xóon	north wind	raspy **h**: **h**oon
x'	x'áax'	apple	(unique to Lingít)
x̱	x̱áat	salmon	scraping back of throat: **x̱**hot
x̱'	x̱'áan	fire	(unique to Lingít)
xw	gáaxw	duck	ki**xw**
x̱'w	x̱'éishxw	blue jay	(unique to Lingít)
x̱w	(du) húnx̱w	older brother	hoon**x̱w**
x̱'w	x̱'wáat	Dolly Varden/trout	(unique to Lingít)
y	yéil	raven	**y**ay (y-AY-th)

LINGÍT VOWEL	LINGÍT WORD	ENGLISH DEFINITION	ENGLISH EXAMPLE (sounds like)
a	at daayí	birch	**A**merica (low tone)
á	t'a	salmon (general)	Americ**a**, w**a**s (high)
aa	aan	town/land	f**a**ll (low)
áa	áa	lake	f**a**ll (high tone)
e	dandewooyaa	marmot	el**e**phant (low)
é	té	rock	p**e**t (high tone)
ei	seit	necklace	g**a**te (low tone)
éi	dléit	snow/white	v**ei**n (high)
i	Ginjichwáan	Canadian/British	h**i**nt (low)
í	hít	house	h**i**t (high tone)
ee	ee ká	room	h**e** (low tone)
ée	neech	shoreline	k**ee**p (high)
u	nukshiyáan	mink	b**u**sh (low)
ú	gút	dime	p**u**t (high tone)
oo	woosh yaayí	pair	gl**ue** (low)
óo	óonaa	gun	b**oo**t (high)

Any mistakes in the Lingít language are mine. Any mistakes in the different Sámi dialects or understanding the Sámi culture are mine. I am a beginning student.

ABOUT THE AUTHOR

Vivian Faith Prescott was born and raised in Ḵaachx̱aana.áak'w, Wrangell, in Tlingit Aaní, Southeast Alaska. She lives and writes at her family's fishcamp next to Ḵeishangita.aan, the old Red Alder Head Village. Vivian is adopted into her children's clan, T'aḵdeintaan, Snail House, and she's a member of the Pacific Sámi Searvi. She holds an MFA in poetry from the University of Alaska Anchorage and a PhD in Cross Cultural Studies from the University of Alaska Fairbanks.

Vivian is the author of nine books, including poetry and short stories. With her daughter Vivian Mork Yéilk', she writes an award-winning column for the *Capital City Weekly/Juneau Empire* called Planet Alaska, as well as co-hosts their popular Planet Alaska Facebook page. Visit her at vivianfaithprescott.com and follow her on Instagram @planetalaska and Twitter @planet_alaska.